STEVEN KEYES

Illustrations by the author

CONJECTURE BOOKS • Los Angeles

.

Cover Illustration by Steven Keyes
Cover Design by Len Smith

978-0-578-80211-4

CONJECTURE
BOOKS
stevekeyesnyc@yahoo.com

*To Leigh Curran and the kids and adults of
The Virginia Avenue Project*

Acknowledgements

I'd like to thank some people who supported and helped bring this book to life.

Andrea Lyman for years of friendship and character; Gwen Feldman and Eddy Espina for invaluable tech skill and knowledge; Matt Barber, Ellen Byron, Susan Champagne, Jay Coughlin, Laurie Graff, Jayne Larson, and Nicole Schlosser for early encouragement and notes; Len Smith for "animating" my cover drawing.

The much-missed Dori Fram and my mates at her table: Neil Koenigsberg, Weslie Brown, Stacey Collins, Jon Dabach, Jody Fasanella, Pamela Hayden, Pavlin Lange, and Mary Ann LaRussa for ongoing feedback (and snacks) during the writing of this book.

And especially in loving memory of Pat Wagner who made it possible for me to write it.

1

The beach at the lake was Danny Dawson's favorite place. Well, the water in the lake to be exact. And under the water to be even more exact. When you're under water nobody calls you names. Or you can't hear them, at least. Under water everything made sense. That's where he was like everybody else. It didn't matter that his hearing wasn't so good. The water gave everything a mysterious sonic glow. And being under water was very relaxing. I guess, Danny thought, that's why fish flap around so much when they're caught. They don't want to leave. And late in the summer afternoon when the sun starts to set and lay on the horizon, it's a big fiery orange ball that almost looks like it doesn't want to go. That it's gonna put up a fight.

"Don't go too far. Stay where I can see you."

His mom stood on the shore, looking out to where Danny and his sister Becky were chasing waves in the surf, trying to beat the tide. The sea foam soaked their sandy feet. Sliding into the ripples, Danny dipped his head then submerged himself completely. When he bobbed up out of the water, his hair was darker, matted and wet. He didn't feel so *red*. Sometimes having red hair was a drag—just another way that he felt different.

Becky ran out of the waves with a seashell. It was long and narrow and looked like a trumpet. Danny followed behind. "Let me listen to it."

"Wait a minute. Me first." His sister drained the water and sand from the shell then held it up to her ear.

"What does it sound like?" Danny asked.

"Nothing really. Like an echo or something. You probably won't be able to hear much." Becky handed him the shell. Danny pressed it against the side of his face.

"You don't have to push so hard. That won't make it any louder." The shell was there, up to his ear and he didn't hear much except that it sounded like someone calling from far away. Danny'd been deaf in one ear since he was a baby. Not totally but enough. When he was two, he had a really bad infection and when he got better, he couldn't hear as good. He took medicine and it wasn't such a big deal. Not a very big deal but big enough for a kid. He'd gotten used to the doctor visits and had memorized the ear chart completely by heart. It looked like a maze and all the parts were connected. He prolly knew it better than the doctor. There was the drum and the hammer and the anvil. It was like having a hardware store in your head. Sometimes his hearing was cloudy and sometimes it was bright. But the water was where he felt free. He couldn't go in too deep or his ears would pop and he always had plugs to keep the water out.

The western border of Ohio is part ways on the eastern edge of Lake Erie. That's the big lake. His family used to be closer when they lived in Ashtabula. It's a funny name for a city but that's really what it's called. Ashtabula is a Native American word that means "river of many fish." When his parents told them they were moving away, Becky got really upset to be leaving her school and all her friends. Danny looked on a map to see where they were going. A place called Milford Haven. It was pretty far, even though things look smaller on a map. Like you couldn't walk or ride a bike there or anything. His family used to go to the beach a lot but then their dad moved his business so it was a whole day trip to get to Ashtabula now. That beach was always his favorite place. Under water everything seemed like a dream. Like being in space or something. You could float and spin like a dancer and practically fly without falling. It didn't matter if you couldn't even swim that good. Danny'd never taken lessons and swam well enough not to drown. Sometimes his mom worried too much so he wore a floatie belt just in case. He had a kickboard, too and his favorite swim shorts—aqua blue with sharks.

"Come on, kids. Get your stuff. We're heading back."

His parents were waving from the top of a dune and ready to go.

Oh well, Danny thought. Becky grabbed the shell and they raced to the car where their parents were packing up for home.

That was the last time they'd been to the beach. Milford Haven was in the middle of Ohio. There were parks and pools and stuff but nothing like the beach at the lake. They'd maybe take a family trip to a museum or the Botanical Gardens or something but the beach at the lake near Ashtabula was still the best thing ever.

2

"Stand on the other side so I can hear you better," Danny said.

Andrea moved over to his left. "Sorry. I always forget you're deaf."

"Just in one ear. On the right. Not completely but it's kinda fuzzy. Muffled."

Andrea handed him the flashlight. "Sorry."

Danny leaned down from where he was standing on his old baby high chair. It had zoo animals all over and some crusty dried strained peaches. Or something. It was kinda wobbly but tall enough to reach.

"He called me Helen Keller once, too."

"Well, that's not a bad thing, really." Andrea always looked on the bright side. "Look on the bright side. Helen Keller was a great and historic woman of courage and wit. Beethoven was deaf and he was a genius—Mark Going is a big jock so he gets away with stuff. I think I heard him fake whisper the

'N' word in the lunchroom once. At least he noticed me. He's really popular."

Danny couldn't believe his good ear. Andrea was his best friend and she was defending the enemy.

"He's a creep and a bully."

Andrea steadied the chair under Danny's feet and continued her argument.

"He *is* your sister's boyfriend."

"My sister's only fourteen. She's too young to have a boyfriend."

"In some states that's old enough to be married." Andrea squinted thoughtfully then asked, "Do you think they *do it*, you know, your sister and Mark? Like make-out, kiss and you know—stuff?"

Now that was just gross.

"I don't know. When he's here they have to keep the door open though."

"I bet they do it in secret anyway."

"Gross! Mark Going is a creep. And a fascist."

"You don't even know what a fascist is, I bet." Danny had heard the word on the TV news and wasn't exactly sure what it meant but it sounded like something Mark Going could be.

Andrea stood her ground. "What is it, huh?" She looked up a Danny without even blinking.

He didn't answer.

"I thought so."

"Well, I'll get a dictionary as soon as we're out of this closet."

"A fascist is like a huge bully who's corrupt, rules countries and is mean to everybody so I guess you're sorta right."

Danny was only almost eleven and Mark Going was graduating from middle school. "He's older so why is he picking on me?"

"That's how it goes sometimes with bullies, you know. It's the law of the jungle. I saw that on *Nat Geo*. The stronger preys on the weaker."

"I'm not weaker—just shorter."

"Well, he *is* a jock. They like to show off how tough they are. You know, impress their friends—all the other jocks and girls. That's just the way it is, I guess." Andrea had started biting her nails again.

"Why do you bite your nails all the time now?"

"I don't know. I think when I get anxious maybe."

"What are you anxious about?"

"I don't know. Life, I guess… My mom says it's 'cause I used to suck my thumb when I was a baby. It's called sublimation. I looked it up. That's when you do one thing instead of something else. She wants me to stop. I might try hypnosis."

"Cool. You should. It's gross."

Danny wanted to find that doll. His mother had put it up here on the Shame-shelf. That's where anything he and his sister weren't supposed to see, have or know about got put. Or just stuff that needed a place to be. Kinda like the junk drawer in the kitchen, only interesting and not sharp when you stuck your hand in.

"Why'd your mother put it up there anyway? It's only a doll. And probably not even anatomically correct..." Andrea said God was in the details. "God is in the details. That's what my grandma says. So, why it is up there?"

"My aunt found me playing with it and told my mom. And then I took it to the family picnic and got grounded so she put it up here." Danny was starting to feel a little light-headed and wanted to sit down and have some juice and about five cookies like when he had a blood test two weeks ago and almost fainted.

"You're really geeking out about this doll." Andrea slid down on her back against the closet wall. She was chewing on her thumb. "Is it like the time you stole your sister's Bratz underwear?"

"I didn't steal it and anyway she never wore them, not once. They were still in the package. I was drawing them for art class, you know—animation week. All I did was copy the pictures."

"Still... it sounds creepy. Drawing pictures of underwear."

Danny aimed the flashlight up and felt inside a shoebox at the back of the shelf.

"Just the pictures, that's all—I got it!"

He pulled the edge of the box and it tumbled down.

Right onto Andrea.

"Ow! Thanks. Kill me, why don't you? It smells in here. What's that smell?" Andrea jumped up with the doll in one hand and a fistful of tissue paper in the other.

"My mom says it's mothballs. To keep the moths away. They eat the clothes and stuff."

"Oh. Well, so here's the famous, stupid doll."

"*Stupid* doll? You're a girl. You're supposed to like dolls."

"You're a boy and *not* supposed to, so we're even. I can't believe this is such a big deal. Most people have better things to do."

"Well then, go do them." Danny was still light-headed and getting irritated. "And stop biting your nails. It's unsanitary."

"Oh, please, Mister Underwear Stealer."

Andrea had been Danny's best friend since she moved to Milford Haven almost three years ago. They'd met at a table during lunch one day and were in the same grade and same homeroom, too. She was taller than Danny by almost a head and always wore one pigtail on the side. She called it her teapot look. And she loved barrettes. Sometimes she'd wear four or five.

"I like mixing the colors around. To make a rainbow."

Andrea held up the doll.

"Here she is. Her hair's a mess, though. You should at least comb it or pin it up or something."

Danny jumped down and smoothed out the disheveled dolls hair.

"I'll do it tonight. Now put the chair back and let's get out of here before we both get caught."

"Your mom can't do anything to me. I'm not doing anything. It's your doll."

At least for now it was. Danny loved it. The life-like features and the details on the pinafore and there were even real eyelashes. His sister had gotten it from their Aunt Helen for her thirteenth birthday but showed only a polite interest which she lost within days. ("A doll? Oh, please.") She found her cellphone much more useful and fascinating. She even named it "Molly" like it was a pet or something. There had been a lot of discussion about this and her attention span in recent months, but his sister's loss was Danny's gain.

"Does she have a name or anything?"

Danny wedged himself against the closet wall, squeezing between Andrea and the laundry hamper. They examined the notorious doll.

"I'd think after all the drama, you'd at least give her a name. She's kinda pretty but it's weird that her nails are painted and she's wearing an apron. She looks like a fancy maid."

"Becky put that nail polish on... I think she's from *The Sound of Music* maybe. That's an outfit like in the movie."

"Let's look her up online." Andrea had been placing phantom bids on eBay up to five dollars. So far she'd never won an auction, which was good because she wasn't supposed to be bidding.

"Maybe she's valuable."

"She's valuable to me," Danny said proudly. "She's beautiful."

"Well, I know all the songs from *The Sound of Music*. We went to the Sing-Along three years ago. You could call her Maria. That's the name of the star. She's the Lonely Goatherd then she becomes a nun. No wait—first she's a nun then-"

"Mark Going called me a Show Queen."

Mark had been invited for Thanksgiving dinner last November and—looking for the bathroom—had mistakenly surprised Danny who was in his bedroom singing "We Need A Little Christmas" from some musical.

"Mostly just 'cause I liked that one song from when that movie with the red-haired lady was on TV."

"Uh, *Lucy*—like from the old show. She was a television icon."

Andrea knew all about TV Land, too.

"My uncle used to call me Dragonfruit," Danny said.

"You sure get called a lot of names."

"That was my nickname. Dragonfruit."

"I've never had a nickname. I like dragons, though. They can be scary but magical, too… I think I've heard of that fruit but I've never seen one."

Danny couldn't believe there was something that Andrea didn't know, hadn't looked up or read.

" 'Cause of my hair. It's a fruit from Mexico. Like a melon and it's all red with prickly points on top. My Uncle Bill gave me a book about it. Rare and exotic, he said. He died."

"Oh, sorry."

"I think I might dye it. My hair. Like black or brown or something darker, more cool than *red*."

Andrea gasped. "Don't do that! You're a 'ginger'. That's who you are. Prince Harry was like a future King of England and he's got a whole bunch of red hair. There's a lot of famous redheads: Lucy, Pippi Longstocking, Bozo."

"Yeah, gee, thanks… And what's a 'Show Queen'?" Danny asked.

"I saw a ballet about a 'Snow Queen' once. *Frozen* is that same story, too. Hmm… Are you, you know—gay?"

Andrea was always full of questions, that's for sure.

Gay. Whoa. Danny didn't know. Why does anybody have to be *anything* all the time anyway? Gay or not. Good or bad, or happy or sad. It seemed to him most people were lots of stuff put together, sometimes even all at once. Maybe that changes when you get older, Danny thought. I guess you just have to wait and see.

"I'm not… I don't know… I think my mom thinks that will happen. That's why she took the doll away. My aunt saw these people on TV who were gay and some of them were boys that had dolls once. I don't know…What's going to happen to me?"

Andrea patted Danny on the head. "Don't worry about it. If you are, you are. My oldest cousin is gay. He's rich and lives in New York so it can't be that bad."

"My dad calls New York 'Sin City.'"

"That's Las Vegas," said Andrea, air-guitaring with a clothes hanger. "Las Vegas is in California and all the movie stars live there." Danny thought about the star of *The Sound of Music* and if she was safe in Las Vegas, California.

Just then they heard footsteps padding up the stairs and down the hall.

It was Becky. Danny could tell when she popped her gum.

They listened as she stopped, pulled the closet door open and peeked inside. Danny and Andrea were huddled in the corner with the doll. Becky stood in the shadow of the doorway, looming over them like a raptor.

"Omigod! I am so telling!"

Andrea jumped up, squeezed past Becky, practically tumbling down the stairs and ran out the front door. "Bye!"

Becky tugged on the light string and peered down at Danny, her eyes flashing.

"You're in big trouble now."

Then her phone lit up. She answered it and turned and walked away.

3

B ob and Janet Dawson had just gotten home from a *Rich Dad* seminar.

"You know that *Rich Dad* is much more good-looking in person." Janet set her purse down on the kitchen table. "I hope his financial advice is better than his picture."

Following behind, Bob hung his keys on the hook next to the coats. "He's supposed to be a money genius, not an actor."

"Well, I've been curious about him. The books are very popular. It never hurts to check something out."

"Seemed like a nice guy, I guess. Popped in and waved but that's about it."

"He spoke for a minute or two."

"Well, we can watch the DVD. I mean, it was free. Maybe we can try it out. Heck, I wouldn't mind being a *Rich Dad*."

"Wasn't that Danny's little friend running down the street…? What's her name? Andrea?—"

The phone rang. "Who's this now?" Bob sighed.

Janet picked up the extension. "Hello."

"Hello, Mrs. Dawson. Is Beck—Rebecca— there?"

Mark Going called Becky "Beck."

"I hope so. Who's calling?" her mother asked.

"This is Mark, Mrs. Dawson."

"Oh, Mark, yes, I'd think you'd call her cellphone."

"Uh—I don't use cellphones."

"Oh. Well, why not if I may ask?"

There was a pause and then silence on the other end.

"Hello? Mark? Are you there?"

"Yeah…uhm… They give you tumors. Cellphones."

"Oh, my… I haven't heard that. Okay. Well, if you say so… I wish you'd tell Becky, maybe we'd get her off it for a minute."

Bob Dawson walked into the living room. "Who is it, Jan?"

"It's Mark—you know, Becky's friend."

"Oh, is she here?"

"Call upstairs, Bob—Mark, I think you should try her cellphone. As long as *you're* not using one, I think you're safe. Just call from, you know, the one on the wall. Where are you now?"

"At home in my Dad's office. You know, down the street."

"Well, try her from there."

"Oh. Yeah. Okay. Tell her I called though."

Janet hung up the phone then said "Okay. Will do" to no one in particular.

"He's got it again!" Becky came bounding down the stairs. "My doll. He's playing with it. It's so embarrassing!"

"Oh my. I put it up in the closet. That's off-limits."

"He doesn't listen. He's obsessed. He's always sneaking around like a spy. Especially at Christmas."

Last year Becky paid Danny three dollars to tell her where the presents were. She said she'd die if she didn't get an iPod.

She didn't and she didn't.

"It was on the shelf. You know you kids aren't supposed to go up there."

"He doesn't pay any attention. He does whatever he wants. Remember my *Bratz* underwear?"

Bob walked in and took a package of pork chops out of the freezer.

"I don't want to hear anything about that ever again. Your brother was grounded for a week."

"He was grounded for the doll, too. But that never works. And why can't I get unlimited minutes on my phone?"

"We're not going through that again. Mark called and-"

Becky stopped him mid-sentence. "Ohmigod—when?"

She ran back upstairs.

"Just now." Janet put the pork chops into the freezer. "We just this minute walked in the door…"

Bob stared at her. "I just took those out."

"Let's get MandarIn & Out tonight, okay?"

"Geez, can't we ever use the oven, even once a week. What's the point?"

"The point of what?" Janet had some knitting to get to.

"The point of having a gas stove. And pork chops that have been sitting in the freezer for a month."

"Okay, well, take them out, I'll do something."

"Where is Danny?" Bob called upstairs. "Can't leave that kid for a minute. What's all this about that doll? I'll take it out back and burn it if this doesn't stop."

He gave a sigh, walked into the living room, sat, pushed back on the recliner and closed his eyes.

"Do you think *Rich Dad* has to deal with this stuff? He probably just hires somebody. Let's call that *Super Nanny*."

"Oh Bob, our kids are too old. We'd never get her here. And besides, those shows are all rigged. *Reality*, indeed. I don't know what it is about this doll that has Dan so worked up."

Bob cracked a smile. "Maybe he's practicing for the real thing."

"You think so? Oh my. Maybe, but this is new. He never played with dolls when he was younger. This whole thing is out of the blue. It's always something, Bob. Our Daniel is an endless source of issues." Janet was working on an afghan shawl in autumnal greens and rust.

"I just hope I can get this finished in time for your mother's birthday. Helen gave me the pattern but it's a little difficult."

Bob shook his head. "I wish we could get a pattern for our son. He's not following directions."

"We should go see his teachers."

"It's not the kind of thing I'm going to talk to strangers about. It's bad enough our family has seen it."

"Just at that reunion picnic."

Danny had brought the doll to the family reunion in his backpack last August and his cousin Tammy had made a scene because she wanted it and boys shouldn't play with dolls anyway and it was a big mess.

"I should've thrown it in the lake."

"That's an heirloom doll from Helen and I'm not throwing it out. We just need to be firmer with him. What if our son is gay, Bob? I mean, it happens all the time."

"Oh, geez. Just 'cause he plays with a doll doesn't mean he's gay. It's a phase. Kids go through more phases than the Starship Enterprise. That doctor show had a program."

Janet shook her head. "You're as bad as your sister. Just because somebody on TV says something, it must be true."

"Alright then, you're the one who hid it. You're the one with the Shame-shelf—Let's forget all about it. Let's just buy him a dress and heels on QVC. I don't want to talk about it anymore. Where is he? Dan!"

Uh-oh. When his father called him "Dan!" it was serious. He strained to hear but always heard that very clear. Andrea was gone and he was on his own. He guessed he'd better stay in the closet a little while longer. The air vent made a good speaker. He could hear them from the kitchen and sound came up the stairs from the living room. It was great practice for listening. He'd gotten really good at what his grandpa called "eavesdropping". You know, what nosy people do. Then there was a new voice. He leaned in a little closer.

"Hey, Mr. Dawson. How are you this evening? Is Rebecca here?"

It was Mark Going. All polite and stuff on his phony 'best behavior'.

"She said to meet her here at the house."

"Hello, Mark, just a minute she's… where is she, Jan?"

"I'm here!" Becky came out of the kitchen eating a Go-Gurt.

"Hey, Mark. How was practice?"

"Okay."

It was April so that meant baseball. Mark Going was the pitcher and during football season he was the quarterback and then there was something called "lacrosse," which sounded very fishy to Danny because they all wore little shorts and pushed a ball around with a stick.

"So you wanna go see that movie?"

Becky stared at Mark, the Go-Gurt tube hanging from her mouth and began to drool. "Sure, whatever…"

Bob dug in the cushion for the remote. "It's a school night. What's the movie, Mark?"

"That one, you know, about the sea captain. He was a real person. A hero even, I think, sir."

Bob turned to Becky. "Do you have homework?"

"No. The substitute never gives any."

"Okay." He looked at Mark. "You can go but be back by nine."

"Sure thing, Mr. Dawson."

"How are you getting there? You need a ride?"

"My brother's going, too. He drives."

"Good. Be careful."

Danny's mother came out of the kitchen. "What about dinner?"

"We'll stop and get something on the way." Becky pulled on her coat, impatient to leave. "There's stuff at the movie."

"Well, it's a school night. Be back by eight."

"Dad said nine."

"Oh, well—okay. But nine on the dot."

"Whatever." said Becky. "And keep you-know-who out of my room."

"Yeah, whatever. Have a nice time." Danny's father waved them off and his mother got back to her knitting. Autumnal colors were very soothing.

* * * * *

Danny was still in the upstairs closet. He thought about maybe never coming out. Crouched into a ball, he wondered how small he could get, camouflaged like a caterpillar or an armadillo protecting themselves in the wild. He curled up and remembered a story he'd read about some people in Asia who paint words and pictures on a single grain of rice. Really. I mean, how small can a thing be? There's microbes and amoebas you need a microscope to see and he'd heard about strands of DNA that are invisible to the naked eye. There's so much in the world you can't see just by looking. How tiny does something have to be to qualify as a living thing? He felt pretty small right now. Then he heard the front door shut. Becky and Mark were gone so he unscrunched himself and decided to go downstairs. His parents were still talking but their voices sounded more serious now. Sometimes you just don't know what's going on with parents. Was he in trouble and getting grounded again? Maybe if he waited long enough they'd forget about the whole thing for now, at least. He wished that he could just do stuff without it being such a problem. What was wrong with liking a doll? It was pretty, like a painting or a statue. His cousin Jimmy played with army man dolls all the time and nobody called him names. Danny hated when his parents got upset. He didn't want to be a trouble-maker. Maybe he could go downstairs and act like nothing happened. Be all fake and innocent like Mark Going. So he took the doll into his room, carefully slid it under the bed, climbed up onto the pillows and blankets, yawned and fell asleep.

4

Mark's head was splitting. He and Becky were sitting watching the movie, this one about pirates attacking and taking over a ship on the open sea. It was supposed to be so good but Mark couldn't concentrate on the screen. What if I have a tumor, he thought. Or an aneurysm even. Ever since sixth grade when they'd had to read that book about a kid who died from a brain tumor, he couldn't get the idea out of his head. It was a sad story and all but, I mean—man, was it depressing! And now these cellphones were igniting everywhere and exploding into flames. Another reason he refused to use them. Plus, there were concussions and stuff, too. He played football and even though he was the starter QB, he backed into the goal line whenever he could. His buddies made fun of him but Becky was like a message service and used the phone enough for them both.

His best friend Kyle Novacek said he was a rebel.

"You're a rebel. Who knows what evil lurks in those monstrosities we have jammed against our ears? They've like done studies. Electromagnetic radiation, it's called. You could be right and outlive us all. Only the years will tell."

Roger Doremus disagreed.

"Get real, man. You might set your hair on fire but you have a better chance of being struck by lightning or eaten by a shark than catching cancer from a cellphone."

Roger and Kyle were in a garage band called **SPAWN** and always trying to get Mark to join. Singing? No way. When he was about five or six or so, his mom made him be in this show, an opera about this brother and sister, Hansel and Gretel.

A traveling company was in town and using local kids for the small parts. He didn't want to but his mom insisted. His mom was really into this musical stuff. She said it would be a good life experience. So he had to wear these goofy shorts with suspenders and a pointy hat with a feather and stand around with a bunch of other kids cheering at the end when the witch got clobbered. Sing in a band? Yeah, that was never gonna happen. And they played too loud. Beats and playlists were cool. That was okay. But the thing of it is, you can't see what's happening *inside your head*, your brain. There's all kinds of stuff going on up in there and who knows what?

Becky stared at Mark. He was wearing those ugly saggy sports shorts she hated, a hoodie and *black* socks with sandals. He *was* cute and super popular but acted like such a baby sometimes. So immature. Older by nearly a year, Becky was born late, the day after cut-off for enrollment and had to wait another year to start classes. She was nine when they moved and had to leave all her friends for a whole new school. It was all so unfair!

"Where's your brother?" Mark's brother Sam had ducked out of the movie to talk with his girlfriend on the phone and had been gone for a half-hour at least.

"He's talking to Heather."

Becky nudged Mark's arm and handed him the popcorn bucket. He ate for a minute. Munching on the kernels, he could hear the crunch of the corn amplified in his head a million times over. She nudged him again.

"What's wrong with you?"

"I have a headache."

Somebody behind them whispered a loud "Shhh!". Becky turned around, rolled her eyes and said "whatever." She paused for a moment then stared at Mark.

"You have headaches all the time. Maybe you need one of those whaddaya call it—X-ray thingees?"

"MRI. I had one last year after I got sacked at that game. I was slammed pretty bad but nothing showed up."

"Well, I hope *something* did… I mean, you've got a brain in there, at least. Maybe you need glasses."

That person behind them gave another "Shhh!", this one louder than the first.

Becky and Mark glanced at each other and then sat silent.

His dad wanted Mark to play football like him. His brother had played all through high school and was now going off to college in the fall to play there, too. His dad said sports was a "Going tradition". He had to be good at something and it seemed that was it. Sometimes he wished his dad would just shut up about family traditions and making a name for yourself in the world. Toughen him up, his dad said. The world's a hard place and you have to learn how to make your way or somebody else is gonna get there first. Where was 'there'? Was it some invisible finish line that only his parents could see? It's not like he was a nerd or gay or some loser or anything. He just wished that his parents would shut up sometimes.

What did he have to prove?

Why can't everybody just leave him alone?

Becky tugged at his sleeve and tried to take his hand. Mark pulled away.

"This popcorn is stale and this movie really sucks."

With that he stood, walked up the aisle and out of the theatre.

5

"Now, I want everyone to remember: your Show-and-Tell presentation is just as important as the item you are sharing."

Throwback Thursday happened at the school once a month. Show-and-Tell was a little kid thing but on Throwback Thursday "we go back to an earlier time. We celebrate our cultural heritage and have some fun, too." Miss Mathers, the homeroom teacher was from Georgia and had an accent that made everything sound like big-time laughs. Her sentences all went up 'happy' at the end. She could report you to the principal's office and you'd almost think it was a party or something. Today, she was dressed in a cowgirl outfit and wearing boots with a bandana around her neck. A couple months ago Danny had brought in what his grandpa called a 'rotary phone'. It was from the olden days, made of green plastic and shaped like a box. You had to dial the numbers in a circle and it took really long. The speaker was attached to a curly cord that got tangled all the time. A lot of the kids in homeroom had seen them before in pictures or movies but never up close.

On Throwback Thursday Show-and-Tell you could dress up as someone from the past or an old TV character or something. Or just sit and watch.

"And please, no talking during your classmate's presentation. Everyone will have a chance to speak. And now Danny will share his item with us."

Miss Mathers crossed to her desk as Danny brought his backpack up to the front of the class.

"Tell us what item you'll be sharing with us, Danny."

"Well, my item is one that my aunt gave to my sister and then I got it."

Andrea covered her face and slid down in her chair. Maybe he should just talk about the backpack, she thought.

Danny unzipped his pack and pulled out the doll. Jennifer Edwards in the first row said "Ohmigod" and Matt Ross said "Whoa!"

Miss Mathers stood up. "Kids, now everyone, let your classmate speak."

Danny straightened Maria's petticoat and cleared his throat.

"This is a collectible doll from the movie *The Sound of Music.*"

"We all know that movie, don't we guys?"

Miss Mathers gave a little clap of her hands. Maybe she's been to the Sing-Alongs, Danny thought to himself as he held Maria up so they could see her in the back. "She was actually a real person who escaped the Nazis and became famous as the head of a singing family."

Miss Mathers raised her hand. "Daniel, I think we all know the story…Why don't you tell us why you chose to share this item with us today?"

Somebody in the back of the classroom laughed.

"Well, I really like how it looks and that it's so realistic."

"Yes, I agree. It's very artistic. And you've kept it in very good condition. Does anyone want to ask Dan about his item?"

Somebody in the back of the classroom laughed.

"Yeah." Matt Ross raised his hand. "Why are you playing with a doll, dude?"

Danny paused for a second and thought. "I don't play with her—it. I just have it. To look at and think about."

"You *think* about it?"

"Yes. About the story."

Matt Ross cracked his knuckles.

"Do you ever think about that you're so gay?"

Jennifer Edwards and most of the rest of them laughed.

Miss Mathers stood up and gave another clap. "Kids, please. Matthew, that's not an appropriate question. This is Show-and-Tell."

Danny smoothed Maria's hair and thought maybe he should've brought his grandpa's stamp collection after all.

Andrea raised her hand and Miss Mathers called on her. "What's the name of the doll?" she asked.

"Maria," Danny said. "The doll's named for Maria Trapp."

"*Von* Trapp" said Andrea helpfully.

"Yes." Nobody said anything or asked any more questions so Danny held the doll up one last time so everyone could see and then carefully replaced it in his backpack.

Miss Mathers stood up, took a breath and said, "Thank you, Danny for sharing your item with us today. Who's next?"

She waited for a response.

Somebody in the back of the classroom laughed.

✦ ✦ ✦ ✦ ✦

"I can't believe you brought her to school. The doll, I mean." Andrea always sucked the straw long after her juice box was empty. She took one final slurp. "I shoulda stopped you. Somebody's gonna get on your case."

Somebody already does, thought Danny. And his name is Mark.

Andrea continued. "And she's not Maria Von Trapp, she's Heidi. I found it on the internet. Heidi's a totally different doll and not based on a real person. She's from a book. I looked it up."

Danny blew into his empty chip bag and popped it but like always, he could never get it to make a noise. He wadded it up and tossed it on his tray.

"Well, okay, I don't care. Anyway, I don't play with her. I just have her. She's a collectible."

"Whatever. But I wouldn't bring her here anymore. Somebody's gonna beat you up. That happens all the time these days."

"Yeah, I know..." She didn't have to tell Danny, that's for sure.

"You need a spirit animal."

"A what?"

Andrea flustered a sigh. "A *spirit animal*. Not a real one. It's symbolic. Like from the Chinese New Year. Me and my parents were at a restaurant over Christmas and they had these placemats with all of it on there. The Chinese have animals for every birthday. Symbols, like a horoscope and every month is a different animal. You can also pick your own."

Danny thought that sounded fun.

"So, what does it do, the spirit animal?"

"It sort of protects you. A good luck charm. Like a four-leaf clover or a rabbits foot. I'm deciding between a butterfly and a panda. I like all the colors on a butterfly and pandas are cute. And *red* pandas are endangered."

"What about a dog?" Danny thought that a dog would be nice.

"Sure. Anything. I love dogs." Andrea sighed. "Our dog Dusty died when I was eight. We never got another one..."

"We can't have a dog. My Mom's allergic."

"Oh. Too bad. Animals you know, have super senses. I loved Dusty. He was special. I think he was psychic."

Danny liked kangaroos, too.

"How do I find out which animal I am?"

"It's all online. I look everything up. When's your birthday? That's how you find out which one you are. I mean, you could pick a dragon like your uncle called you. That's a good one, I bet. Dragons are super popular. They're all over the place on TV and movies…"

"That's actually not right."

Danny and Andrea looked over and saw the girl who said it.

"You know—what you said about spirit animals."

It was a girl from seventh grade. Her name was Karina Sampson. She leaned over to their table.

"You know I'm part Native American, right? My dad is full-blooded Cherokee. Spirit animals are a Native American thing. It's part of the culture. My parents told me all about it. My meemaw—my *grandma,* was a shaman…"

Karina was a grade ahead of Danny and Andrea said she was really pretty and had lots of boys around her all the time.

"She's really pretty, I think. Like movie star beautiful."

A shaman is like a—well, Danny wasn't sure so he asked Karina.

"What's a shaman?"

"A shaman is a tribal leader, a seer who's in touch with the spirit world and can see into the future and make the sick well again."

Karina flipped her head back and pulled her hair into a bun then stuck a pencil in it. Her hair was jet-black and shined in the light. She wore a beaded string on her right wrist and a copper bracelet on her left. Copper has healing powers. Danny'd read that in a magazine at the dentist's office once.

"I heard you talking. You're right about the spirit animals but it's not Chinese. Spirit animals originated with—are a big part of—the Native American tradition. My dad's from a tribe in Tennessee. Wolves are the most popular spirit animals."

Andrea was uncharacteristically speechless then said "Well okay" and offered Karina her hand. "I guess you'd know better than me."

Karina looked at Andrea's hand then gave her a fist bump. "I don't shake. Who knows?—you know, germs and stuff."

Then Karina stood up and walked away with her tray. "Later…"

Danny thought about changing his spirit animal to a wolf and Andrea wondered why Karina was sitting alone.

"I mean, she's so beautiful and everything."

"Maybe she just wanted to be by herself."

"If I was that pretty, I'd *never* want to be alone… So when's your birthday again?"

6

"Ohmigod, Mom. It's mortifying! He brought it to school. When I heard I couldn't believe it. Everybody's talking. Thank god I wasn't sitting in that classroom. I'd of died. My brother brought a *doll* to school. My doll."

Becky was in the kitchen microwaving a pizza roll. Her mom was sitting at the table with the laptop.

"You didn't want anything to do with that doll."

"But it's still mine. He brought it to *school*. You should hear what people are saying. Newsflash: my brother is a freak!"

"Don't say that. That's a horrible thing to say."

"Well, why does he do it? Tell me."

Janet inhaled a breath then said "I don't know. I don't know what to do. He seems to be very attached to that doll for some reason. We've been through all this before. Let's not tell your father, okay?" She gave a sigh. "Where *is* your brother, by the way?"

Becky shrugged then laughed. "I don't know. Check the upstairs closet."

"Don't joke. He's your brother. It's getting late and starting to rain." Janet poked at the keypad with her finger. "I want to get this done before dinner. Can you help me, please?"

The timer on the microwave beeped and Becky popped it open.

"What are you trying to do?"

"I'm on one of these websites to send my teaching application out."

"You're going back to teach?"

"That's the plan."

Becky reached over and tapped some buttons on the keyboard.

"Let me see your teeth, Becky." Janet peered at Becky's mouth. "Smile for me."

"What?"

"Smile and let me see your teeth."

"My teeth? Mother, please! Not this again. I don't need braces."

"Well, you'd be lucky if you didn't. Now just let me see…"

Becky stood to her full height and thrust her chin out, smiling dramatically.

"Okay? How's that?"

"Good. Nice. I just want to make sure you're taking care of your teeth."

Becky rolled her eyes. "I would never have braces. Ohmigod Mother, please. I would die."

"If you need them, you'll get them. We'll see what the dentist says."

Becky tapped **Enter** on the keyboard and stepped over to the counter.

"There you go. There's your app."

She grabbed her snack and walked out of the kitchen.

"I'll be in my room."

Janet sat focused on the computer screen. She swiped, clicked a button and said "Viola!" as a message popped up that her document had been sent. She felt brilliant.

Then the knob on the kitchen door squeaked open. Danny hoped no one was there. His mom was sitting with her back to the door so he tried to sneak past but she turned around and stopped him.

"Well, speak of the devil and he shall appear. I was just about to send out a search party. Where have you been, young man?"

"Nowhere. School. I just got home."

"I can see that. It's after four o'clock."

"It is?"

"And what's that under your jacket?"

It was raining so Danny'd left his backpack inside the porch and had Heidi under his favorite blue jacket. It was baggy and loose and had lots of pockets to hide things for protection.

"I asked a question. What have you got under there?"

"Nothing."

"Daniel William Dawson, stop right this instant. I heard all about your day at school. There was some sort of Show-and-Tell?"

"Yeah, I guess."

"Well, is there something you want to show and tell me?"

Danny stood frozen in the spot then pulled up his jacket and took out the doll.

"She's called Heidi."

His mother just shook her head and said "What are we going to do with you?"

At the moment, Danny didn't have any suggestions.

"And you're dripping wet. Go dry off. We'll be eating dinner soon. Do you have homework?"

"No. We had a pop quiz today."

"How did you do?"

"Good. It was on that book."

"Which book?"

"This one about a kid."

His mom looked confused.

"Oh. *That* one…What was it about? The story. How was it?"

"Okay. It's about this kid who gets sent away to camp and has to dig holes."

"What did you think?"

"I thought I hope I never have to go to a camp like that."

Danny's mom laughed. "You and me both." She wagged her finger. "But please: behave…Where are you going now?"

"The garage."

"The garage? What's out there?"

"My bike."

"It's raining. You're not going back out in the rain. What's the matter with you? Your bike? That bike's been sprouting cobwebs."

His grandparents had given Danny a big fancy bike for his birthday when he was nine and he rode it into a woodpile at the end of the alley because he couldn't figure out the brakes. He wasn't wearing a helmet and he split his head open and there was blood all over the place and it was the last time he rode it. His mom was really aggravated.

"You know the rules. You're not to ride it without a helmet and since you refuse to wear one—well—I think your bike can wait."

"I just want to put some new stickers on it. I'll stay inside, I promise."

"Stickers? Well, if you're out there I'd think you'd want to help your father by doing some of those chores."

Danny's two chores were to check that the recyclables were in the right bin and to sweep out the garage. He used to help his dad shovel the driveway in the winter. Everything was always buried until the spring but then they got a snow blower and didn't have to do that anymore.

Becky's chores were straightening her room which was always a mess and keeping the upstairs bathroom clean—neither of which she did with any regularity.

She was always "super busy."

Danny couldn't figure out with what and their mom and dad had stopped trying. They talked a lot about hormones and 'adolescent angst'. His dad said teenagers were God's revenge for a misspent youth.

"I'll just go out for a few minutes and come right back in, I promise."

"Oh, alright. Just don't be all night. Come in when I call. Dry yourself off while you're out there, too. And I'll take that doll, if you don't mind."

Danny set Heidi on the table and went out to the garage.

He didn't really have any stickers so that was a fib. He wasn't supposed to tell a lie but he liked to be in the garage all alone when it was dark. And even better when it rained, especially if there was lightning or thunder or both. Danny would turn his bike over upside down and play spinning wheel. That's the only thing he used it for anymore. He didn't ride it. Not if he had to wear a helmet. He didn't like anything on his head. Not a hat or a helmet or anything.

He'd go into the garage and pretend he was an evil troll like that character Rumplestiltskin spinning gold from straw and casting magic spells. He would turn the pedals so the wheels spun. Churning the bike faster and faster then stopping it really quick by jamming on the brakes, Danny skidded his hands along the tires. Then he'd do it backwards the other way. He laughed and imagined his mortal enemies being scrambled between the spokes and begging for mercy. Tossing his head back, he laughed like a manic cartoon villain, vowing vengeance and cursing his foes. He was invincible, all powerful and could never be stopped.

He was a big deal. A Master of the Universe.

Then his mom called him for dinner.

He turned the bike over, set it aside and went back into the house.

7

Some of the flyers were bright yellow and some were hot pink. They were posted all over boards in the halls and Miss Mathers was handing them out between periods. It was about tryouts for the Spring show. Danny remembered last Christmas when he was in the pageant.

"Back home we call them *pantomimes*". Alistair Coombs was an exchange student from England for three months last year. He talked very fancy, called everyone "lad" and "chap" and was an experienced *equestrian,* he said. That meant he could ride horses and not fall off. He was the narrator in the Christmas pageant and Becky thought he was a "dreamboat", good-looking and stuff. Mark Going didn't like that but they'd only been going together since September and Becky said he was being insecure.

"Grow up! Alastair has a passport."

He said he rode horses every weekend and that in London there are foxes running around the streets all over the place like squirrels in the park.

America was ruled by England until some of the people got sick of being bossed around and fought the Revolutionary War against the King and won. That's what the Fourth of July is about. Independence and freedom from oppression. Danny thought that lately all he'd like to do was get away from his sister and her boyfriend, for a start.

Alastair knew all about history, too. History means everything that happened before you were born. Even your parents have history like when they were kids and stuff. Danny couldn't imagine his parents ever being kids but I guess everybody has to start somewhere.

"I'm doing a video history of my family." Andrea said she was going around asking all her relatives about their lives and she even had a name for her movie company. "PBJ Productions. That's short for peanut butter and jelly, my favorite food after bacon. I'm documenting my ancestry on an old camera my Dad gave me. It has playback and everything. So far I have six hours of footage. That's a lot but I'll fix it in post." *Post* was what happened after everything was done, how you put it all together. And also a cereal company.

Danny was supposed to bring the Spring show flyer to his parents but didn't want to get involved so he folded it up and put it in his pocket.

"Hey, you!" Danny was at his locker when he heard what sounded like Mark Going's voice. Or was he just imagining things? "Bernadette!"

Nobody was there. The monitor wasn't anywhere around. The hallway was deserted except for some kids hanging out down by the windows. Then he saw Mark Going.

"Bernadette Peters!"

Why is he calling me *that* now? Danny thought to himself. He tried to act deaf in both ears, which sometimes worked at home.

"You're the Queen of Musical Comedy, right?" Mark was standing directly behind Danny who was almost two feet shorter and could feel Mark's breath on his head.

"Who's Bernadette?"

"Ah, come on Show Queen, don't pretend you don't know."

"I don't," Danny insisted.

"Yeah, right—She's you!"

"Why don't you go pick on somebody who cares?" Danny couldn't believe the words had come out of his mouth. Emboldened, he turned, looked up at Mark and said "I don't know what you're talking about."

"Well, maybe you need to look a little harder and you might see Broadway stars."

Danny stepped back, closed his eyes and wished for Instant Super Powers.

Then Mark put his hand on Danny's head and shoved him down into the open locker. He slammed the door, which banged off Danny's shins and said "Bye, bye, Bernadette."

Danny felt like a Whac-A-Mole or Alice when she went down the rabbit hole in that book his grandma had given him last Christmas that he never finished.

"Hahaha," Mark laughed like one of those people on a talk show when something wasn't funny and walked away. "Bernadette, the Show Queen!"

Wedged inside his locker in a sitting position, Danny stared up at the He-Man poster on the door, squirming to get himself free. Two older girls walked past, looked down at him, giggled "Potty training?", flashed screen shots with their phones then continued down the hall.

Bernadette, the Show Queen? Danny would have to Google this Bernadette and find out who and what Mark Going was talking about. Or maybe Andrea knew.

"I know she's a big star. She played the witch in *Into the Woods*."

Danny remembered that show because the fifth grade went to see it on a field trip last year.

Andrea continued. "But not the one we saw. The big one on Broadway a long time ago. She wasn't in the movie, though."

"Well, I don't know why he called me that and my neck still hurts. Should I tell my parents?"

"Tell your sister. Maybe she'll dump him."

"No. She'd prolly like that he pushed me. She's on his side. And besides, he's too popular. That's all she cares about."

"Nobody's *too* popular." Andrea bit down on her thumb. "And I do think it's weird that Mark Going even knows who Bernadette Peters is. That's kinda gay. I mean for a jock and everything…"

"There might be guys who aren't gay that like musicals." Danny didn't really like them that much, either.

Andrea rolled her eyes. "Possibly. And I might be Michelle Obama. All I'm saying is that this whole situation is very shady. Maybe he's a closet case." She whispered this last phrase in her secret inside voice.

Danny was puzzled. "Like a closet with a Shame-shelf?"

"No. Not a real closet. Like a secret place where people hide who they deep down really are. If you ask me, Mark Going is a hot mess. My cousin says closet cases are all hot messes."

"The one who's rich and lives in New York?"

"Uh-huh."

Sometimes Danny's Aunt Helen would bring what she called a "Dump Cake" over on a special occasion holiday. She poured everything into a pan, mushed it all together, and then put it in the oven to bake. He thought that might be like what a "hot mess" was.

"Sort of, I guess. If people were cakes. My cousin says lots of actors and politicians are and that most of them live in La La Land."

"Is that near Las Vegas?"

"Uh-huh. Only worse."

The pass bell rang. Danny grabbed up his backpack. He and Andrea had to run. They were late to dreaded fourth period Math.

"I hate Maaaath!" Andrea sang as they sprinted down the hall.

"But I looooove lunch!" Then the second bell rang.

8

The bus home was not too crowded, which meant everybody got a seat to themselves. Danny sat in the back. He still felt pretty bad from the whole incident with Mark. And those girls had tweeted that picture of him crammed inside his locker. Double humiliation! All you could really see were his knees but still he was angry and mad and glad to be alone. Who needs people?

Stella Ong moved to sit across the aisle from Danny. Stella was going to Bejing China that summer to visit her grandparents and attend junior pre-Olympics gymnastics camp. She was also in swim club and a straight-A honor roll student. She was a brainiac, but not obnoxious about it.

"I wanted to tell you that I liked your share in homeroom last week. I'm a big *Sound of Music* fan, too."

"Oh. Thanks. But I found out she's not that person. She's—it's from a storybook. And anyway, I'm not really into dolls, you know-"

"You just liked the story, like you said…"

"Yeah."

"Maybe you'll be a writer."

"I don't know."

"Do you want to sign my collage? It's for Earth Day. Happy Earth Day!" She unrolled a poster and passed it over to Danny. It had cutout pictures of places all over the world, with a big sun in the middle and clouds and hearts pasted on. "Here's a marker. Use this to sign."

Danny was feeling grumpy and not in the mood for any capital-D Day, Earth or otherwise. "What should I write?"

"Anything you want. You could say "Happy Birthday, Earth!" or something like that."

"Okay." Danny wrote

Happy Birthday, Earth. Keep up the good work.

After he wrote it he thought it was stupid but put the cap on the pen and handed it back to Stella. She read it and said "'Keep up the good work', that's funny. You have a good sense of humor."

"Thanks."

They sat there for a minute then Tommy Kessler walked back and sitting in front of them, stretched out with his legs all over the seat.

"What's up?"

Tommy wore these glasses with really thick lenses.

"I have a stigmatism. I can't see too far. At first I didn't like having to wear them but I got used to it and now I don't mind too much. My grandma says they make me look *distinguished*."

Tommy was also like the only kid at school who didn't have a backpack. He carried a briefcase instead. Danny's grandpa had the same kind and when he was little they used to play "businessman". Tommy's was brown and flat with latches by the handle. He had transferred from another district last fall and some kids used to make fun of him carrying a briefcase— being new and all, but he didn't care. He did it anyway 'cause that's just the way he was. If you keep doing something long enough, it's the way you are and maybe people stop paying so much attention and leave you alone.

Tommy set the case on his lap and clicked it open. Then he took out a deck of cards and started shuffling them.

"I play gin, poker and bridge. Never for money so it's not gambling or anything. Sometimes I let the other person win—as a gesture of good will. I can also do some magic. Wanna play? I could teach you. I've been to Vegas. Twice."

Stella sneezed but Tommy always had his headphones on so he didn't notice. He hardly ever played any music, he just liked wearing them, he said. "You can hear what people are saying but they think you can't. Tricky. Like in poker."

Tommy's agility with his cards fascinated Danny.

"So, whaddaya wanna play?"

"My Grandma taught me Go Fish and Animal Rummy. Those're the only games I know."

"Those are baby games. I can teach you grown-up ones…
So?"

"But my stop is coming up and I'll have to go…"

"Okay, well, no worries. Maybe next time…"

Tommy straightened his cards, slipped them in the box
and carefully placed the deck into a pocket of his briefcase.
Then he took out a bag of chips and pulled it open.

"Want one?"

Tommy could practically eat his body weight in food and
never get fat.

"I have a very high metabolism. That means I won't get
fat. I have twenty hamsters. Eighteen are babies. Hamsters
eat their young so we had to separate them. Like my parents.
They're divorced. I'm going back in June to visit my dad in
Toronto. That's in Canada. Their national symbol is the
maple leaf."

Tommy had had a near-death experience two years
ago when he choked on some gummy worms and lost
consciousness for almost ninety seconds.

"I didn't see white light or anything like they say. I just felt
really tired when I woke up then they gave me a popsicle."

Tommy liked to talk when he wasn't eating.

"I'm very verbal. I score off the charts for verbal skills. You
know my favorite food? Large portions!"

He laughed and looked at Stella who was not amused.

She stood up and grabbed her bag. "This is my stop."

Danny kinda liked her okay. She brought him back a
paperweight when she went to London last year.

She told him "That's a bust of Shakespeare."

Andrea said she thought Stella had a crush on Danny.

"I think she has a crush on you. Somebody doesn't just bring a paperweight from England to a kid they don't like. You're crushable."

Danny wasn't sure if he even wanted a crush.

Andrea batted her eyes and whispered "Stella—that means starlight in French or Italian or something… I'll have to look it up. *Crush-able!*"

9

Danny sat at the kitchen table across from his mother who thoughtfully folded, unfolded then re-folded the hot pink school flyer.

It was almost origami now.

"I found this in your jacket. What's it about—a show at school? Will you be involved?"

"There's singing." Danny hesitated. "I can't sing in a show. I'm deaf in one ear."

"You are not deaf. You're a little hard of hearing on that one side. You are mildly *hearing impaired*. The doctors said it was not a necessary surgery. As long as you take your medication, you're fine. I think doing this show would be good for you. You've been onstage before. You were lamb or a sheep in that Christmas pageant last year."

"I was a goat." That Christmas pageant was lame. All the kids had to be in it and everybody had to have a line to say. It was supposed to be a big event.

Do You Hear What We Hear?— Sounds of the Season

Ugh! It was big alright. It shoulda been called Do-You-Smell-What-We-Smell?

The music teacher Mr. Van Horn kept farting during the whole show.

"He's got acid reflux. I heard him talking," Andrea whispered. "It's like gas that comes out one end or the other as either farts or burps. A lot of old people have it."

His mom continued. "Go. Try out. Maybe this one will be fun."

"And anyway," Danny protested, "I don't want Mark Going to have any more reason to torment me. It's bad enough already. All I need to do is start singing."

"Mark? That boy who sees your sister?"

"Yeah, him."

"He bothers you? What does he do? Does he pick on you?"

"Yeah, pretty much."

His mother scowled and her eyes flashed. "Well, that's not good. Why didn't you say something?"

" 'Cause Becky already hates me and—"

"Your sister doesn't hate you. Don't be ridiculous. It's just all that business with the doll…"

His mother's voice trailed off as she got up and poured some coffee.

"I'll have your father talk to this Mark boy."

"Please, don't."

"He shouldn't be making you miserable. At school or anywhere. If he's a bully… well, I don't want your sister going anywhere with a bully."

"Mom, please don't say anything. It's no big deal."

"Well, it's a big deal to me."

Danny snatched the flyer from the table, unfolded and shook it, waved it around then stuffed it into his jacket pocket. "I think I will go to this tryout."

"What?"

"I think you're right, Mom. I do want to go to be in this show." Danny cracked a fake smile. "I like to sing!"

"You do? Well, that's good. I mean we've really never heard you sing but you have a nice speaking voice. When you were the sheep-"

"Goat."

"Okay, goat."

"They had too many sheep and I wasn't big enough to play an ox. So I was a goat."

"Well, when you were the *goat* a number of people mentioned your voice."

"All I said was 'Three kings from the east!' and then 'Baaaaah' a lot."

"Is that what a goat says?"

His mother was wearing him out with all these questions.

"I don't know what a goat says but they sound like sheep and Mr. Van Horn said it didn't matter unless there were farmers in the audience."

"Your grandmother grew up on a farm… I guess it might matter if you were Meryl Streep. Or Meryl *Sheep!*"

She laughed at her own joke and took a sip of coffee.

"But you're right. I think you should go for it. You need to get out more. I worry about you."

"Don't worry, Mom. I'll go."

"What's the name of the show again, that they're doing?"

Danny took the now crumpled paper flyer from his jacket pocket and smoothed it out on the tabletop:

Milford Haven Middle School
Presents

A Spring Broadway Musicale
Tribute to the Great White Way

AUDITIONS
COMING
SOON!

"Oh, that's what they call it, the Great White Way."

Then she reached for the hot pink flyer and knocked her cup all over, soaking everything in coffee.

✦   ✦   ✦   ✦   ✦

"I can't believe you're trying out for that musical. You're sure brave. I would barf." Andrea and Danny were on the computer in his bedroom and she was surfing the net. There were parental blocks but you could still see enough cool stuff.

"Don't you have stage fright?"

"I don't think so. I didn't mind that Christmas show too much. My Mom wants me to and besides, if Mark Going is gonna call me 'Bernadette Peters,' I might as well go for it."

"Shhh, look here. There she is. I Googled her. *Bernadette Peters.* Maybe you'll do one of her songs. She sings a lot of 'Sondheim', it says. He's a big deal musical writer. Famous." Andrea was reading from the internet. "She's the *'premier interpreter of the Broadway songbook.'* Wow. Look... she's a redhead, too. I don't like her hairstyle, though."

The picture on the screen was a little blurry but she looked fine to Danny.

Andrea turned and blinked coyly.

"So, what are you gonna sing, Bernadette?"

"Shut up, don't call me that."

"Okay, sorry but you have to try out. Do you know any songs?"

"Only Christmas songs and 'Happy Birthday.'"

"You know, every time anybody in the world sings "Happy Birthday," the lady who wrote it gets paid. It's called 'copyright infringement'—like stealing—if you don't pay. She invented the song." Andrea was becoming an expert legal mind. For eleven, at least.

"And you should never copy anything and say it's yours 'cause that's stealing, too. It's called 'plagiarism.' And, what if you copy something that's crummy—well, then I mean, what's the point?"

"Thanks, maybe you should become a lawyer."

"Maybe I will. The ones on TV get paid a lot more, though. And a lot of them are fake."

"Well, what should I sing? I need to take music or a CD to the tryouts."

"My cousin in New York left a whole bunch of music in our basement when he moved. He used to be a singer but now he's a 'hedge-hog.' That's what my Dad calls him. He manages money for rich people. We can look for some songs."

"Okay, I guess." Danny clicked off the computer. As their reflections glowed on the screen, Bernadette Peters faded to a shiny blue.

10

When he was seven, Danny and his Uncle Bill set up a lemonade stand on the sidewalk in front of the house. His uncle said that it would help Danny to become an *entrepreneur*. That meant someone who starts their own business and makes money. Like raking leaves or babysitting.

Some kids sell cookies and candy and stuff. His dad said he had a paper route when he was younger but nobody really does that anymore.

Adults were always talking about what was going to happen when you got older like them and how you had to be prepared.

Danny got kinda tired of hearing it.

He missed his Uncle Bill and his imaginary friend. Imaginary friends were a baby thing but when Danny was four he was still sort of a baby so he invented one. The names were on the labels of apples at the grocery store and he called everything Pippin and McIntosh for a long time and then made up an imaginary friend named Mr. Pippin McIntosh who was a big apple with shoes and hands like Mickey Mouse.

Danny used to make a tent with his bed covers and talk to Mr. Pippin McIntosh about stuff before he went to sleep. About how he was feeling or a TV show he saw. Mr. Pippin McIntosh never spoke but was a good listener. When Danny got older, he and Mr. Pippin McIntosh didn't talk as much and then one day Mr. Pippin McIntosh just kinda went away. Danny still missed him sometimes especially at night or in the morning before breakfast and school.

Later after Mr. Pippin McIntosh, Danny used to think when he grew up he wanted to be a kangaroo but was disappointed when that turned out not to be an option for a human kid. That's why he liked his backpack. Kangaroos could keep everything in their pouches and get away fast but also totally kick anybody who got in their face. So he always carried his backpack and sometimes thought about running away from home. Once, when he got grounded he tried but got chased back by a German shepherd at the end of the street.

At night sometimes when it was quiet, he'd lay awake in bed and listen to the trains passing from miles away, the wheels rolling on the tracks and the horns blowing warnings. He'd wonder about the people who were riding in them and where they were going and what their lives were like. And if the moon was full he could see it through the curtains. It looked so far away but still so close. It never seemed quite real. Spaceships landed there. Astronauts walked on it. Incredible! That something so far away could be gotten to. It was brave to do those things. Be an astronaut and stuff. Danny wondered if he could ever do something like that. He didn't like being high up. And it would be easy to get lost in space. He got lost one time at a mall when he was five but was too young to be scared. This lady at a store took to him to an office. He wasn't sure what was going on but they made an announcement and gave him a candy bar then his parents came and got him.

When you're little, you think that your parents will just always be around. When you're little, you get scared of stuff but when you're older, other things can scare you.

When you're little, you just don't really know too much. There was 'stranger danger' that his parents told him about so he didn't go around talking to everybody that he didn't know. But getting lost might not be such a bad thing, though. Sometimes getting lost can be an adventure, too. You might see something you hadn't seen before or end up somewhere new. Like an explorer. Danny always kept some snacks in his backpack just in case he was stranded in the wilderness and had to forage for food and live by his wits against the forces of nature. You never knew what was gonna happen. Look at Tommy Kessler's hamsters. Maybe a lemonade stand was a good idea, just in case.

11

"Beck please, you know I don't like cellphones." Mark Going was finishing off one last game of Halo and waging Armageddon interstellar war against The Covenant.

Becky pushed the phone into Mark's face.

"Oh, come on. Just say 'Hi' to Misty, she doesn't believe you exist."

Misty was Becky's best friend who had moved away to New Mexico last year.

"I don't wanna. Leave me alone."

"I guess I'll just have to tell her my boyfriend is a wuss who is afraid of cellphones."

"Shut up!"

"Don't tell me to shut up. It's true."

She spoke into the phone.

"Sorry Misty, he can't talk right now. He's busy trying on my underwear. Gotta skurt. I'll text you later. Bye."

She tapped the phone and jumped onto Mark's back.

He shrugged her off. "Why'd you tell her that? Who's Misty anyway?"

"Why do you care? If you wanted to know, you could've talked to her."

"What's that noise?" Mark stopped mid-Halo and stuck his nose in the air like a startled deer on *Animal Planet*.

Becky stopped to listen.

"I don't hear anything."

"Singing. I hear singing. That song from *Grease*."

There was rhythmic thumping coming from down the hall.

"That's my brother's room. He's got his friend over. That dorky black girl from sixth grade."

"Why are they singing?"

"Who cares? Maybe they're practicing for America's Next Top *Nerd*. Now shut up and rub my neck."

✦ ✦ ✦ ✦ ✦

"I'm not doing 'You're the One That I Want' so don't start singing it again. It's for two people, anyway."

"That's called a *duet*." Andrea was humming the song now. "That means 'two.'"

"I don't like this one..." Danny picked up some music, looked at the title and tossed it aside. He was feeling very selective. If he was gonna make a fool of himself, he might as well not sing a stupid song.

"They sang these all the time on *Glee*." Andrea was losing her patience. "You are 'hyper-critical,' and that's not a good thing."

She had dragged the whole bag of sheet music all the way over to Danny's house so the least he could do was consider her suggestions.

"What about this one: 'What'll I Do?' by Irving Berlin. I think he was a big deal composer in the olden days."

They read through the words carefully.

"It seems kind of sad: 'When I'm alone with only dreams of you… what'll I do?'"

To Danny, this was the kind of song that made his grandma cry.

"It's sad. I don't like it."

"God, you're so picky. Just sing something you know," she pouted, "or get a karaoke CD or something."

"I think the words are important."

"Here. Look at this one."

Andrea handed Danny a song called "You Gotta Be a Football Hero."

"Oh, very funny, yeah—I'm gonna sing a song like this."

He read the words: "You gotta be a football hero to get along with the beautiful girls… Oh, great. Maybe I should just go in there like Mark Going and act all tough."

Andrea's eyes lit up. "You should. It would be funny. It's better than 'Happy Birthday.'"

Danny had no idea what she was talking about.

"Why would it be funny?"

"Because. You sure don't look like a football player."

"Well, it's a 'jock thing' and that's not me."

"Right. You're not a jock. You're the opposite so that makes it funny."

Danny thought for a moment.

"And besides, how do we know what the music sounds like?"

"Duh. We can download it. There's like every song ever made on the internet. We could do it tomorrow."

"Okay. I guess we could hear it. But I'm not wearing a helmet. I don't like anything on my head."

12

"I've got to get back to those scrapbooks. These photos are a mess." Janet had spread out a whole shoebox of family pictures on the coffee table.

"Do you think scrapbooks are obsolete? I mean with everything online nowadays—does anyone even do this anymore?"

Bob sat across from her reading the newspaper. "I don't know. Why am I reading this paper? I could see it all on TV or the computer. I like to hold something in my hand—and besides, I do the cross-words, too."

Janet held up a faded, tattered photo. "Oh, my goodness— look at this. It's your brother Bill in his Boy Scout uniform. May he rest in peace."

"Yeah," said Bob. "Good old Billy. He had to go jump off that cliff."

"Bungee jumping they call it."

Bob shook the newspaper and turned the page.

"Billy was always the risk-taker. World traveller, wild child. The prodigal son."

"But, why in the world…?"

"He was celebrating his Big Four-O. What a way to go, right?"

Janet shook her head. "That day was a nightmare. Thank God none of the kids were there. But your poor mother…"

"What's it been? Three years now?"

"Next month… He was always making jokes. You know, it bothered me when he used to call Dan Dragonfruit."

"He was kidding. It was a nickname. Billy was always giving everybody nicknames. We all had 'em. I was the 'Sigh-Master,' remember? He said I always sighed too much."

Bob took in a deep breath then let out a huge siiiiiiiiiiiiighhh.

Janet was not impressed. "I don't see what's wrong with sighing. It's a natural function of human respiration. It's healthy."

"Billy always thought I was being dramatic." Bob sighed again then shook his head and chuckled. "Our kids make me look like an amateur in that department. Nicknames. We all had 'em."

"That's not the point. I don't like name calling."

"Look honey, Dan was Dragonfruit 'cause he's a redhead. So is my sister Helen. We have a couple of redheads on my side."

"Well, it bothered me. I don't like nicknames and I think Daniel has been a little hurt."

Looking away, Bob turned a page.

"It was no big deal. Kids get over stuff. And Billy's gone now. The whole nickname thing kinda evaporated. I think

Dragonfruit has been retired. Nobody calls him that anymore, do they?"

"Well, you know that boy Mark, that boy Becky sees, Dan says that he bullies him."

Bob sighed. "Oh, geez. When did you hear this?"

"Danny told me a few days ago. He asked me not to say anything but we need to talk with that boy's parents right away, I think. I'll over go to the school, too. The principal should know about this."

Suddenly, Becky ran into the house slamming the front door.

"They can't do this! It's so unfair!"

"Oh, boy—here we go again." Bob flipped his lounge chair upright.

"Now what?"

Becky stomped through the living room past her parents.

"Rebecca. Becky. What's wrong?"

"Oh, Mother. Nothing. Everything. It's just so sorbid!"

Sorbid? Was that a word?

"What happened, honey?" Her mother had never heard the word "sorbid."

"I think she means *sordid*," Bob said. "You know—sleazy, *drama*—like on a daytime show."

Becky wheeled around to her father. "Whatever!"

"What happened?"

"Oh, just the worst, most lame thing. That principal is a d-bag!"

Becky's mother had never heard the phrase 'd-bag' and was afraid to ask.

"Hey, young lady! Watch your language in front of your mother."

"Oh, Daddy... And right before Prom, too!"

It seemed Mark Going had been caught vaping with two buddies in the school basement and was now banned from any and all extracurricular and sporting activities for the rest of the year.

"Vaping. You know, electronic cigarettes. I mean they're not real or anything. And who cares if he's wearing a ninja bun. It's his hair!"

Apparently 'ninja buns' had become a fashion must among the athletes during the current baseball season.

"I just can't believe this could happen. My life is over!"

Becky stalked out of the room and up the stairs, slamming her bedroom door.

"Oh my. I've heard about this vaping. A lot of people do it but the school's no place for it. Right, Bob?"

"Another fancy way to get in trouble. I remember smoking in the locker room back in the day-"

"I've never seen you smoke."

"Well, I didn't like it but I did it in high school. To be cool. I used to rub Cheeto dust on my fingers to look like nicotine stains. Smoking was what the cool kids did. And cigarettes were hardly the worst of it..."

"Cool? Well, I hope neither of our kids ever feels the need to be *cool*."

"*All* kids feel the need to be 'cool.' It's a rite of passage. We're lucky if smoking is *all* our kids wind up doing."

Bob let out a sigh as he eased himself back into his chair.

"Wait till they start with the tattoos..."

"Don't even say that!"

"Well, I have a tattoo, remember?"

"Oh, that little shamrock on your shoulder?"

"Yeah."

"Well, you were younger—and Irish. You always had to do everything your brother did. These kids..."

"Everybody has tattoos nowadays."

"Well, I don't like them. And they're permanent. If you want to remove them you can't."

"You can but it's painful."

Janet chuckled then shook her head, "When I was thirteen I dyed my hair green."

Bob flipped the newspaper at the fold and stuffed it into the seat cushion. "There you go. All kids do stuff like that. Like I said, it's a rite of passage."

"Well, I think we need to have a talk with them both." Janet sat down, gave a sigh and then shuffling through the stack of photos, held up a picture of Danny dressed for Halloween.

"Look, remember? He went as that Pokey Man, that Japanese cartoon. I searched everywhere for that pattern and all that yellow felt cost a bundle... He looked adorable though... Bob, I'm thinking of going back to teach. At the community college. The kids are older now and I miss it. I know your business is doing okay but that *Rich Dad* scared me. I just think about the future and you know, I worry."

Janet looked over at Bob for an answer, but he was fast asleep.

✦ ✦ ✦ ✦ ✦

Auditions
for the Spring Musicale

**SIGN UP WITH YOUR
HOMEROOM TEACHER**

ALL ARE WELCOME!

Oh no, Danny thought. It's really happening, I'm actually doing this...Okay...

He stood at Miss Mathers desk and closed his eyes thinking it wasn't too late to back out when he heard her voice:

"Well, Daniel. I'm so happy to see that you'll be coming in to sing for us!"

13

It was Pizza Friday in the lunchroom. "Ugh! Vegan." Andrea scowled as Danny finished off a slice.

"This new 'Healthy Life' menu sucks. Even the mac and cheese tastes funny." Andrea was a committed carnivore.

"Matt Ross brings bacon and pepperoni sandwiches, and he's Jewish. Does that mean I can bring hot dogs on Kwanzaa? I just wish they'd give us Jell-O or something. I mean, back in fourth grade we at least had pudding cups, you know?" She sighed. "It's a new world."

They sat for a moment then she announced, "I've decided my next movie is gonna be called "It was a Dark and Stormy Night". That's the first line from my favorite book *A Wrinkle in Time*. Have you ever read it? You should. It's amazing!"

Danny didn't know that one. "I just read *Holes* for a book report."

Andrea squealed. "Oh! I read that one *years* ago."

Danny was anxious to tell her what song he had decided on when his sister walked up to their table.

Ignoring Andrea with a grimace, she stared down at Danny.

"I hope you're happy. Mom told the principal that you said that my boyfriend is beating you up and bullying you and now he's in *more* trouble. Thanks so much."

Then Becky picked up the second slice of pizza, licked it, and tossed it back on Danny's plate. "Yeah, thanks a lot, Dragonfruit."

She turned on her heels and sauntered off and out of the lunchroom.

Andrea looked to Danny. "That was weird. Your sister is thug. She just licked your pizza and called you Dragonfruit."

Danny stared at the limp and newly gross slice of pizza.

"I told my Mom not to say anything. Now it's gonna get really bad."

"He could get permanent detention. Maybe they'll suspend him or make him do summer school," Andrea suggested. "Except being suspended is like a free vacation, you know?"

But Danny could barely hear her as his heart pounded in his good ear.

✦ ✦ ✦ ✦ ✦

"Use the whole surface. Draw off the page."

Mr. Oates was the art teacher. This week the class had been studying architecture. Building design and interiors. 'Blueprints' are what the designer draws from. Measurements and stuff.

"Why are they called blueprints?" Andrea was at a table behind Danny because she got to class right at the second bell.

"I was powdering my nose." she whispered breathlessly. "I don't like to say I'm going to the bathroom 'cause then everybody knows your business. Powdering my nose is a more polite way to say it. It's a euphemism..."

So anyway, a blueprint is called that because the paper it's on is usually blue.

"Due to the mix of chemicals ammonium and potassium that are used to treat the paper" Mr. Oates explained, "the result turns the paper a light shade of blue."

So, a blueprint is like a map that architects draw up for the builders to follow. There's also lots of different materials they use in construction, too. All kinds of wood and stones for fancy new houses and steel and concrete for really tall buildings and skyscrapers in all the big cities. Making a building is a lot of work. When Danny got impatient for something to happen or be finished, his dad always said "Rome wasn't built in a day." Rome is this city in Italy that, I guess Danny thought, took a long time to build.

But today the class was drawing free-form designs. Different patterns and stuff. Free Form Friday, Mr. Oates called it

"Use your imagination. No boundaries. 'Fortune favors the bold.'"

Mr. Oates was pretty cool. He was also the art club sponsor and married to the assistant principal who was another man. His being gay was a big deal when he first came to the school but now everybody pretty much thought it was okay except for a few of the parents who were always complaining about something. Bobby Bates' mom and dad had threatened to sue the school district to get him fired but that didn't happen and then the whole family just moved away. Danny liked Mr. Oates but wondered if he got called names, too. You can't really call adults names or stuff without getting in trouble except on TV. Why was it alright for kids? Danny wondered if he could sue Mark Going.

Mr. Oates was walking around the tables looking at everyone's work.

"Very good, Dan. I like your use of color and the patterns are unusual. Nice free-form."

Danny decided he liked free-form 'cause you could do whatever you wanted and didn't have to stay in the lines like coloring books. It was kinda like swimming in the lake. You could go in any direction and you wouldn't fall or hit a wall or anything. The first time he went in the water, he was kinda scared. He was only three and wasn't sure what to expect. It all looked dark and endless. His dad said it was okay to be afraid of the dark because it doesn't last forever and sometimes you just have to go for it. Danny wrote down that saying Mr. Oates had just told him so he'd remember it:

FORTUNE FAVORS THE BOLD

He thought it meant that you should be brave. Or braver—but wasn't quite sure so he'd look it up later. He knew that when they got the fortune cookie after eating Chinese food, you could crack it open and the fortune would pop out. Usually Danny'd just eat the cookie but sometimes he read the little slip of paper. And sometimes he and Becky or their mom or dad would both get the same one.

GOOD NEWS WILL COME FROM FAR AWAY or STAND IN YOUR OWN LIGHT AND MAKE IT SHINE. His favorite was YOUR FUTURE LOOKS BRIGHT.

He looked down at the paper and his hand had kept drawing even while he was thinking. It didn't look like anything you'd recognize, like a horse or a tree or anything. It looked weird but Mr. Oates said that was good. That was 'art'. *Weird* can mean different and unusual but not really bad. He stared at what he'd drawn and kinda liked it. Then he thought that one day he might like to be a painter or artist when he grew up. Maybe he could get paid to draw. Who knows?

14

"Dan, quit flipping those channels. Pick one and leave it or turn it off."

Danny liked to quick-change the channels and do a mash-up of all the Saturday cartoons. His dad sounded irritated and it was still early.

"Sometimes I think you have that A.D.D."

Danny had heard Tommy Kessler's dad talking once about his mom.

Tommy's parents had been divorced last year and were always fighting.

"Tommy's dad said his mom has Obsessive Repulsive Disorder."

Bob began to laugh. "I guess that's why they got divorced, right, Dan? Obsessive repulsive. Funny."

Danny had never seen his dad so amused.

"Now what's all this about a bully? Your mother said-"

Danny continued to channel surf.

"Stop fidgeting. We'll get one of those spinners if you want. And turn off that TV! Pay attention to me."

Danny clicked off the remote and his dad continued.

"Now what's all this about a bully?"

"I told Mom it was no big deal."

"Well, if this Mark, this bully is hanging out with your sister it is. I mean, does he beat you up?"

"Well, he just kinda bothers me, pushes me and calls me names."

Danny fiddled with the remote and wished he could go to his room.

"That sounds like a bully to me. Your mother spoke to the principal, Mr. Farber."

"Oh."

"And we're not having your sister see this boy, this Mark, anymore."

"Oh."

"So if he starts anything with you just tell us and we'll take care of it, okay?"

"But what about Becky?"

"We'll deal with her. She'll do as she's told."

His dad sounded like one of those police shows or an old gangster movie.

"I guess it'll be okay now. Thanks, Dad."

"How about you come down to the lumber yard with me some Saturday? You've never seen the new location. We're going 'green' down there. Installed solar panels, a whole line of bio-degradables. Gotta keep up with the times. So, some

Saturday—we can hang out and have lunch and you know...
hang out. Maybe play catch or something."

Danny and his father had never even watched a baseball
game on TV much less played catch. This is more serious
than I imagined, Danny thought.

"Sure."

"You know that we care about you. You know that we love
you, Dan, right?"

"Yeah, Dad. Thanks."

Bob let out a sigh. "Okay then, just so you know. We can't
have bullies running around bothering our boy, right?"

"Right, Dad."

Danny wondered if his sister was going to start tormenting
him this weekend or maybe wait until Monday...

15

And now it was Monday again. Danny hated Mondays. The weekend ended and everything at school started all over. Everything like Mark Going. And math.

Outside the gym, Stella came up behind Danny, tapping him on the shoulder.

"Hi."

Her mouth was covered with a pale blue surgical mask and her voice was muffled. Danny was still kinda nervous around Stella ever since Andrea said he was her crush.

"Why are you wearing that mask?"

She pulled it down. "Oh, it's an experiment for my science lab. I'm wearing this for a week and then checking my carbon levels for any trace effects in my blood oxygen."

"That sounds pretty intense."

"Yeah, my grandparents in China are preoccupied with smog levels and want me to wear a mask all the time but our region of Ohio is an industrial valley and the pollution levels vary. This city has fairly clean air. Compared to China, at least."

Danny was impressed with Stella's knowledge and commitment to her project.

"Besides, there's all sorts of stuff floating around. Bacteria and such. Someday soon we could all be wearing masks."

Danny didn't want to think about that.

"I don't like anything on my head. Or my face."

"So you'd make a bad airline pilot."

"Yeah, I guess. And I'm not crazy about flying in planes, either. But I liked to play Peter Pan when I was a kid. That kind of flying's okay."

"Well, you have a good imagination. You like stories. Like I said, maybe you'll be a writer."

"Thanks, I guess. I don't know what I'll be exactly."

"I heard you signed up for the Spring Musicale. You can sing, too? You're multi-talented. A hyphenate."

Danny had no idea what *that* was. It sounded like a mutant space creature.

"A hyphenate means that you have creative talents in many fields."

"Okay. Thanks for the paperweight."

"Sure. That was *so* last year." She laughed. "Well, I have gymnastics. I'll see you."

"Okay. Bye."

Crushable. Oh, brother…

16

"He does *so* want to go to college." Becky was defending Mark Going to her parents in the midst of a family discussion. "He'll probably get a sports scholarship. He wants to study to be a conversationalist. You know, protecting the environment and stuff."

Her father let out a huge sigh.

"You mean *conservationist*. I wish you were doing better in school, young lady. That's another reason-"

"I can't think. I'm too upset—Mark does not distract me from my studies. He's smart. He even ran for Student Council last year. He helps me."

"Well, he's been bullying your brother and your mother and I don't want you to see him anymore."

Becky spun towards Danny who was sitting on the couch.

"So, how does he *bully* you? I've never seen it. Tell me."

Danny avoided her glare.

"Well, he calls me names and pushes me into the lockers."

"I call you names but it doesn't mean anything. 'Sticks and stones,' like they say-"

Their mother interrupted. "Any kind of name calling is not a good thing, from you or anyone else. It's all bullying."

"Bullying! Ohmigod, I can't believe you are all being so dramatic! He doesn't mean anything. Everybody does it."

"We don't care if everybody does it. Everybody shouldn't do it. You kids should know better. You're older. Set an example. This kind of behavior is unacceptable and your mother and I don't want you to see this Mark boy anymore. OK. End of discussion."

"Are you seriously kidding me right now? No! I can't believe you people. I am so out of here!"

Becky stormed past them and ran out the front door.

"Bob, go after her. It's getting dark."

"Let her cool off. What's wrong with you?"

His parents looked at Danny.

"Are you crying? Oh, Dan…"

Danny was curled up on the couch clutching a throw pillow.

"Are you gonna get a divorce?"

"Of course not. Whatever gave you that idea?"

"Well, everybody's fighting. And you went to that counselor…"

"Counselor? What counselor?"

"Two weeks ago. That guy."

"*Rich Dad*," his mother said.

Bob looked puzzled. "I don't understand."

"*Rich Dad* isn't a marriage counselor, Dan. He's a financial—a *money* advisor."

"Are we poor?"

His dad gave a small laugh. "Not yet."

His mother sat on the couch and stroked his hair.

"No honey, we are not poor. But it never hurts to pay attention to your money. When you're older you'll understand."

His dad pulled him up and swung him around to the floor.

"There's nothing to worry about, okay? Now how about we go out and track down that sister of yours?"

17

"Happy! Happy!
Singing! Singing!
Happy! Singing!
Smiling! Smiling!
Happy! Happy! Happy! Happy!
Smiling! Singing!"

Danny was standing on a stage. It was dark. He couldn't see anything. Then he heard these voices. These voices saying "Smiling! Happy! Singing!" He opened his mouth but nothing came out, there was no sound. He felt that pounding in his ears.

Then all his stuffed animals popped out onto the stage behind him, smiling and singing and doing this crazy happy dance. They were all there: Woody and Buzz, Pikachu, Curious George, Kanga, Kermit, Winnie-the-Pooh. SpongeBob and a Smurf. But they were not his stuffed animals at all. And it wasn't a happy dance. They were marching like zombies and rocking back and forth, stomping their feet. The echo throbbed on the floor of the stage. Their eyes were red and mean and their faces were all snarly and sinister. The singing got louder and louder and then all the toys started chanting his name and pushing him to the edge of the stage. His sister Becky was in the front row laughing and pointing and shouting "Loser!" Mark Going was there, too.

The voices got louder. He fell off the stage into a dark, black pit. He kept falling and screamed for help.

Then he woke up.

What was that, he thought.

It was a dream. A bad dream. All his toys were creepy—singing and dancing and everything had an exclamation point! Like a scary movie was in his head.

When he'd gone in to sing at the tryouts for the show, he wasn't really nervous. He just went because he told his mom he would. He'd listened to the song on YouTube and practiced it over and over in his room. The day of the audition, he stood outside in the hallway with some other kids and waited to be called. Then he went in and sang the song. It wasn't any big deal even though he had only been a goat. He'd decided to go so he went. But now he was getting nervous.

He'd never had a dream like this before.

Once on TV, he heard a lady talking about dreams and how they were the door to your unconscious. So what did this mean? Danny didn't think he had an unconscious but it must be something everybody has.

Do animals have an unconscious?

Danny loved animals. Sometimes more than people and lately a lot more. His grandma had a schnauzer named Maggie but his mom was allergic so they'd never had a dog of their own. His grandma used to say that D-O-G is G-O-D spelled backwards, and it is. She said dogs give "unconditional love." Danny wondered what that was.

His friend Harold who used to live next door but moved away had two dogs that were brother and sister. They didn't look anything alike and were different colors. One was big and one was little. They got along great. Danny didn't see why everything was such a problem. If dogs could get along what was wrong with him and Becky?

Andrea listened intently as Danny stated his dilemma.

Then she had an answer to it all.

"Sibling rivalry. That's what it is. I don't have any brothers or sisters but that's a big thing in families with kids. It happens all the time."

Andrea said she'd always wanted a brother or sister. Danny sometimes wished he was an only child.

"An only child doesn't have older sisters and doesn't have to share."

"But having a sibling teaches you how to get along with other kids and living in the world and stuff. That's what my mom says anyway…Well, maybe not kids like Mark Going. That guy's a big narcissist. It's all about him. A narcissist, you know—stuck up and snotty. 'Me, me, me.'"

Danny thought for a moment and that sounded about right.

"And I guess you're maybe a *liiiittle* scared about doing that show, after all." Andrea said. "You really do need a spirit animal. And fast."

Danny had decided. "I decided on my spirit animal. I'm gonna have it be a dragon. I read about dragons and they're really cool and popular and magical like you said. And I liked that movie, too."

Andrea agreed with his choice if she did say so herself.

"And also, you had a lot of practice with your nickname, so that's good."

"Wouldn't it be neat if I could breathe fire on Mark Going and make him disappear?"

"Yeah. Vaporize him!"

This new revelation made them both walk a little faster on the way to lunch. It was grilled cheese sandwich day.

"Hooray!"

✦ ✦ ✦ ✦ ✦

There is an old story—a myth—about Saint George and the dragon.

In this story, Saint George was like a saint and a knight who fought the dragon and killed it in battle with a sword. I guess this dragon was bad but there are good ones, Danny thought. Dragons could also protect people. Princesses and castles and stuff. So every bad thing has a good side, too.

Danny wondered if somebody like Mark Going had a good side or if he was just bad all the way through.

This book said Saint George was a real person but if he was a real person and dragons are only pretend then was this Saint George guy up made up, too?

"Who knows?" said his dad. "And there's nobody left from Medieval times to ask. They have those ads on TV all the time. You know, that restaurant. We went to the one in Chicago once. Your uncle Bill and I jousted in the parking lot—with plastic lances from the gift shop. Fun times."

18

"So, what song are you doing?"

Andrea was on the edge of her seat. Literally. She was sitting on the chair at the desk in Danny's room and kept pushing the cushion back so she wouldn't fall off. "I can't wait to hear it."

The day after the auditions everybody pretty much got in the show, except this one kid who cried the whole time he was singing. Now they got to pick out songs and Mr. Van Horn would make the final decision of who would sing what. Danny had narrowed down his choices to a song from the show *Seussical* called "How Lucky You Are" and "Never Never Land" from *Peter Pan*.

"I was Peter Pan three years in a row for Halloween."

From the ages of six to eight Danny had been obsessed with the whole Peter Pan mythology. His parents had tried to talk Becky into dressing up like Wendy or Tinkerbell but given a choice between the two, she preferred Captain Hook if anything at all. Never Land seemed like a cool place though, even if it wasn't real.

"I know that one," said Andrea, "but the other one I never heard of. I can't believe you decided without me. I thought you were going to sing the 'Football Hero' song?" She looked a little hurt.

"Well, I sang that in the tryout but they said it wasn't from a Broadway show."

"Where's it from?" Andrea asked.

"I don't know. Some guy just wrote it, I guess for football games—so… you helped me a lot but I don't know, I just wanted to decide for myself."

Danny pulled out copies of the two songs and laid them on the bedspread.

"How will you make the final decision? This is exciting."

Andrea hopped off the chair and picked up a sheet of music. "Where did you get these?"

"On the internet like you said. There's a website. I printed them out."

Andrea looked through the sheets then plucked one out and held it up. "What is this?—This is Bernadette Peters!" She pranced around and was practically singing. "You printed out a picture of Bernadette Peters. *Superstar Crush!*"

Danny grabbed the photo from her.

"Yeah, well, so what? I like how she looks. I think she's pretty."

"Is she your *muse?*"

"What's that?"

"Your inspiration. Why you do something. Like that famous painting 'Mona Lisa.' She was the artists *muse*."

"I don't know. I just like the picture. It's no big deal. Can I sing the song now?"

"Okay, okay. Let's hear it."

Andrea flopped onto the bed with her back against the head board, folded her arms and waited, staring at Danny.

"You don't have to stare at me."

"Well, you better get used to it 'cause that's what people do when you sing. I heard even the big stars get nervous."

19

"Can you believe it—that they're making me do this?"

Mark Going was seriously bummed.

"It's horrible. Haven't you been punished enough?"

Becky was outraged and supportive and pulling her hair into a scrunchie.

"It's like community service or something." Becky shook her head and rubbed Mark's shoulders as they sat side by side in their favorite booth at Sonic.

"You might as well be picking up trash on the side of the road. I can't believe they can make you do this. Isn't it illegal? Maybe you can talk to a lawyer."

"Yeah, right. No. It's the school, it's their call. My Dad said that it's not a legal matter. It's the school's policy and they can enforce it at their discretion."

Becky kissed him on the cheek. "I love when you talk like that. You are so smart."

"Yeah, right."

Mark looked at her like a sad, droopy dog.

Becky paused for a moment then nudged him. "And what's this whole—who's 'Bernadette Peters' anyway?"

"What?"

"Bernadette Peters. My brother says that you call him names—Bernadette Peters."

"I don't know. Some random lady I saw singing on one those musical shows my mom watches. She's big on Broadway they say. She's got all this red hair—it's just a joke. Who cares? I can't believe your brother—it's only a stupid name."

"Well anyway, don't call him that—don't do any of it anymore."

Mark scowled. "Alright, okay? I've got bigger problems now. I have two weeks to learn a song. This is serious. I don't even sing at birthday parties."

"Well, I know all the words to 'Heart and Soul' and I can play it on the piano. OMG, I swear—I get my learner's permit next year and I swear the minute I can drive I will be so out of here. I've had it with these people—Can you believe they *forbid* me to see you anymore, like some sort of, whaddaya call it—uhm, we talked about it in history class— you know—they do it a lot in the Middle East... you know, like the car... Kia?"

"Fiat."

"Yeah, that. We can't even be seen together. That's why I had to meet you here."

"It's no good. It's just no good." Mark Going held his head in his hands as Becky popped her gum, said "Smile. Hashtag: 'I hate parents!'" and took a selfie for Misty in New Mexico.

* * * * *

"Can you believe it? They're making Mark Going sing in the Spring Musicale. *Now* who's the Bernadette?" Andrea laughed.

She and Danny were hanging upside down on the Jungle Gym. The park was deserted. Ever since the new play zone opened near the library, none of the kids used this one anymore. The teeter-totter was rusted and didn't teeter or totter. The grass was overgrown with weeds. This old park was just sort of there.

Mark? Singing? "Where did you hear that?"

Danny felt all the blood rushing to his head.

"I heard your sister telling that goth girl, you know the one who wears black all the time, ditches gym and has two first names—Meredith Meredith. How crazy is that? Two first names…"

"Well, Meredith is a last name, too." Danny said. "And she likes to be called M&M."

"Like the candy?"

"No. That's her initials and she likes that guy, that rapper."

"Okay. Anyway, it was between classes in the hall. She gave me a dirty look, too. Your sister, I mean. I don't know why she's all mad at me. I didn't do anything to her."

Suddenly a bee landed right on Danny's nose, leaving a big sting. His hand slapped his face.

"Ow. Ow. Ow!" He yelled in pain and Andrea slid off the monkey bars.

"Oh no! You just got stung!"

She shooed the now gone bee away.

"Don't touch it! Let's go. My mom's maybe home. She's a doctor, remember?"

Andrea grabbed Danny's hand, pulled him off the Jungle Gym and across the park to home.

The bee sting was really hurting. "Don't touch it!"

Andrea's house was three blocks away and had an infamous history. It wasn't haunted or anything but the people who owned it before them had painted it red and white checkerboard. The dad worked for a dog food company and said it was good advertising. Everybody in the neighborhood hated it and when they finally left Andrea's parents moved in and painted it over in blue and white. It was a great house. It wasn't like any of the others in the neighborhood. It was older looking with turrets on two corners, a real fireplace, an attic *and* a basement.

"That's some sting." Andrea's mom was a pediatrician and her dad was an actual rocket scientist. Really. Like at NASA, only in Ohio.

"Hold still honey, while I get some tweezers." Mrs. Wyman went into the bathroom. "I'll be right back."

Andrea sat by anxiously in an old barber's chair. You could pump it up and down and spin. "It was my Grandpa's. He had his own shop in Alabama. During the Civil Rights Movement he marched at Selma. It's a family heirloom. It's antique." Mrs. Wyman returned holding tweezers, cotton balls, and a box of Band-aids.

"Let's wash that off. I'll need the calamine lotion. Andrea, go get that. And quit biting your nails!"

Danny felt like he was on a hospital show and those were the biggest tweezers he had ever seen. He tried to look at his nose but all it did was cross his eyes. He took a breath and held it.

"This might hurt a little... You're not allergic—you would've had a much worse reaction. Hold still—you're a big boy, right?"

Then Mrs. Wyman said people could go into "animal plastic shock" from a bee sting. Danny had gotten a shock plugging in his Scooby Doo nightlight once when he was six so it was good he didn't have to sleep with a light on anymore.

"I think you heard me wrong, honey. It's *anaphylactic* shock. That's a very bad reaction to a sting or cut. But your version is much more clever." She laughed. "I'll call your mom when we're done here. You know bees love redheads, did you know that? We're not sure why. Maybe because you're so sweet. Maybe that's why you got stung."

Danny blushed red.

"And now your face matches your hair."

Andrea's mom paused and wiped her hands.

"But we need the bees. They're important to our world's eco-system. We have to co-exist. You know—share the planet, get along."

Andrea ran back with the lotion.

"Here you go. It's a good thing we were so close. Lucky."

"Yeah, thanks Mrs. Wyman."

The lotion stung a little but Danny was glad to have the stinger out. Andrea's mom wiped his nose and put a Band-aid on the tip.

"There you go. Take care. Remember the skin is our largest organ."

Danny had never heard that before. He turned to Andrea.

"Did you know that?"

"Yeah. It's bigger than your heart even. But just spread out all over."

Andrea's mom chuckled.

"The heart is a muscle but that's one way to put it. Maybe you should start wearing a hat, young man."

"He doesn't like anything on his head." Andrea was picking at the jar of cotton balls. "I guess he's, uh—*hat-aphobic* or something."

"I hope you at least use some sunscreen with that fair skin. And those freckles. What do you do in the winter? This is Ohio. It gets cold."

"I don't mind ear muffs too much and there's a hood on my parka."

"And he does have lotsa hair." Andrea turned to her mom who laughed.

"Okay. Well, just be careful and try not to scratch. Now let's call your mom."

20

Matt Ross bobbed up behind Danny at the bus stop the next day.

"Whoa dude! What happened to your nose?"

Matt could and would ride his skateboard onto any flat surface and was always appearing out of nowhere, doing moves, popping wheelies.

Danny's nose had swelled a little, turned a darker shade of pink and still hurt. His dad said sometimes things hurt when they're healing.

"What's going on, dude? Your sister's like all totally radical. She shaved her eyebrows. Extreme! Does your family have issues or what?"

He flipped the skateboard into his arms as the bus pulled up.

In a show of solidarity and support for Mark and as a peaceful protest against the punishment heaped on her boyfriend by the heinously bureaucratic school administration, Becky had shaved her eyebrows completely off. This sacrifice, though not unnoticed, had little effect on Mark's case, however. In addition to the extracurricular suspensions and mandatory participation in the Spring Musicale, he was requested to apologize publicly to Danny and anyone else he had been bullying at the next school assembly. So far no one else had come forward but Andrea knew of at least two other victims.

"They're afraid to come forward. Fear of retribution. I saw it once in a movie about jury tampering. But your sister looks like a Manga character. Freaky."

She pronounced it 'Mon-Ja,' which Danny knew from a Bugs Bunny cartoon is Italian for 'eat.'

"It's not Mon-Ja, it's Mon-Ga. Japanese graphic comics."

Danny was pleased he'd finally stumped Andrea.

"Well, you know what I mean. She looks scary."

"Do you think my nose will be okay before the musicale?"

"That's two weeks away and it already looks better."

"Why aren't you in the show? You like to sing and stuff."

Andrea had been so involved in choosing a song for Danny that he wondered why she hadn't signed up.

"I only like the Sing-Alongs. You know, where everybody else is singing too and you can see the words. I think I'd faint or something if I had to do it alone in front of other people up high on a stage. You're braver."

Danny scowled. "I don't feel braver. And now I look like a clown." He wanted to scratch so bad but didn't want to disturb the Band-aid.

"Don't worry, it'll be gone before the show. I wonder what song Mark Going is gonna sing."

21

"Okay, people—settle." Mr. Van Horn stood at the front of the music room. He was the choir director, 4-H Regional Conference leader and faculty advisor to the Chess Club. A lot of the older kids called him "Mr. V" for short. Danny only knew him from being the goat and there were so many people in the Christmas pageant that he never even remembered Danny's name. So he called him "Red".

Everybody who was singing in the show was there for rehearsal except Amber Tucker who had been kept home sick after exhibiting flu-like symptoms. It was the first time they would all be seeing each other sing. One good thing about doing the show was that you could get out of class for practice.

"I'm sure you have all been working on your songs at home, right people? And remember to leave any electronics in the basket on the desk. No phones or pads or pods allowed. I don't want to see any skateboards. And no snacks in rehearsal. Focus, people!"

Suddenly, the doors swung open and Mark Going rushed in carrying a baseball bat.

He stopped and stood there for a minute, looking all frazzled and out of breath.

"Well, Mr. Going, nice of you to join us. Now if only we were doing *Damn Yankees*, you'd have it made. Please leave that bat by the door. This is a peaceful gathering."

"I was—we were—my buddies and me were-"

Mr. V held up his hand. "I know. 'Practice makes perfect'. Let's hold that thought… please just take a seat. Now, you all know Mrs. Cooney. She'll be our accompanist."

Mrs. Cooney worked in the office, taught piano part-time and was very proud to be a *Mrs.* She even had a sign on her desk that said *Les Mrs.*

"Musical theatre is the poetry of America."

She loved musicals and being married, in that order.

"No *Miss* or *Ms.* for me, thank you very much. It took me twenty years to find my *Mister* and I want the world to know!"

She wore sweaters with her initials on the front, even in the summer. Some of the kids called her "Looney Cooney" but she was always nice to Danny.

"And since Mr. Going is joining us late in the process we have a change in the program."

Mr. V took out some sheets of music, looked them over then handed a stack to Mrs. Cooney. "Unless you can offer any suggestions, this is the song you'll be singing, Mark. Please come up to the piano."

Danny couldn't believe how scared Mark Going looked. He shuffled to the front of the room like he was walking the plank.

It made Danny smile a little to see Mark so nervous.

Then Mr. V pointed at him to come up to the front of the room. "Dan Dawson. Yes, you." He pressed a finger to his nose. "Please join us, won't you?"

Well, at least he didn't call me "Red," Danny thought to himself, and no farts so far. But what's going on? He hoisted his backpack and started to the front of the room.

"Leave the pack where it is."

Danny dropped it by his chair and took a place near the piano.

"I'm adding a number to the show. A duet for you two."

Danny's mouth dropped open and then turned dry. He could feel the blood rushing to his nose where the bee sting throbbed.

Duet. That meant two.

He was going to have to sing in this show with his arch enemy?

Together, on stage at the same time?

Why were they doing this? Hadn't he suffered enough?

Haven't I suffered enough? Mark Going thought to himself.

His mouth dropped open and then turned dry.

Not only were they making him sing. On a stage. In front of people. But now he was gonna have to do it with his girlfriend's goofy kid brother who'd ratted him out in the first place.

Any threat from a cellphone seemed a distant memory now.

Why was this happening? It was his worst nightmare. Everything was getting so gay.

Mr. V shuffled through the music and handed them each a copy of the song.

"We think this will be a good thing for you both given the current—uh, situation. I want to see some team work."

Danny looked at the music sheets and couldn't believe his eyes. It was the "Football Hero" song that they had told him he couldn't do because it wasn't from a Broadway show, like anybody would care, and now they were giving it to Mark Going to sing.

"Now Mrs. Cooney will play through it once and we can record it on the computer—a *link*, I think it's called—for home practice. And you'll have to get together for some outside rehearsals. Okay, boys?"

Danny stared at Mr. V, who just stared back...

22

Every day it was the same. The boys in third period gym had to stand and wait to be picked for a team. Danny always wanted to teleport to another dimension during phys ed. Today it was basketball. He stood at the end of the line with Felix Santiago and tried to pretend he wasn't there. It was torture.

Felix had a seizure disorder and wore a helmet to prevent any head injury especially during sports. He also had to wear protective goggles and a mouth guard just in case he passed out and fell. Some of the kids called him "The Fly," but he had a sense of humor about it at least. "*Una vez tuve una fuerade de la experiencia del cuerpo no podia volver a!*" ("Once I had an out-of-body experience and then couldn't get back in!") He never said much but could really crack you up when he did. A few of the taller boys were always chosen first. Then the choices gradually dwindled until the last picks, which were usually Felix and Danny unless there was a new transfer student.

When everybody was on a team they had to form a circle and warm-up by tossing the ball back-and-forth. Then the teams would face off, Coach would throw the ball in the air, blow the whistle and the game would begin. The boys fanned out onto the gym floor, grappling for position. Danny always stayed at the edges of the foul line close to the bleachers where he thought nobody ever looked. His nose was still sore and itchy from the bee sting but Coach said there was no reason he couldn't play since he wouldn't be using his nose anyway.

Danny had developed his own secret method during basketball. He bobbed around a lot to make it seem like he was involved and interested when the whole time he was really staring above the basket at the clock on the wall that had a wire cage over it, I guess to keep it from getting broken. I wish I had one of those on my face like a Super Villain and nobody could punch you without smashing their hand or hit you in the head with a basketball and—oh no, the ball is coming at me, somebody threw the ball to me and I caught it and now I have to do something.

He could see Matt Ross yelling and waving. Danny hopped a little and frantically dribbled the ball. He dodged a couple guys but everything was a blur then he stopped, looked for the basket, closed his eyes and threw the ball up in the air as hard as he could just to get rid of it—

There was an endless silence as the ball hit the backboard and circled the rim of the hoop. It spun and spun—

And then it went in!

He opened his eyes and couldn't believe it.

It went in!

He actually made a basket!

Wow.

He had never made a basket before and it wasn't even on purpose.

A couple of the other boys gave him fist bumps and then kept on playing. Danny stood for a minute, feeling amazed and happy. He was exhausted and excited but embarrassed 'cause he felt like crying so he wiped his face with his t-shirt and went back to the game.

✦   ✦   ✦   ✦   ✦

Outside the locker room after phys ed, Danny and Felix saw Mark Going coming at them from down the hall, talking to a bunch of girls on the way to lunch. Danny wanted to go up to him and get in his face and say "you-think-you're-all-that-and-I-just-made-a-basket-so-there." But Mark walked right past without even looking then Matt Ross came up behind Danny, thumped him on the head and gave him a high-five. "Kudos, dude. A basket! You crushed it! Awesome. Have an apple."

"Thanks." Danny took the apple and told himself that it was only a game but was pretty happy anyway and wished the whole world and his parents could've seen it. He felt proud and cool and all that good stuff. He felt like he was someone else.

23

"So you and this Mark boy are singing together? Well, I think that's nice and a good way to put all this behind us. And I'm glad to see that nose is clearing up. A bee sting is no fun. Let the healing begin, as they say... I'm not sure who says it but it's a good phrase."

Danny's mother continued to work on her knitting project.

What started as a shawl over the past few weeks had become a blanket.

"I guess I just couldn't stop. It's very relaxing and look at it now."

"Grandma will sure be warm." Danny wanted to brag a little.

"Mom, I made a basket today."

"In your arts and crafts? That's nice. Is it here? May I see it?"

"No, Mom. A basket in basketball. In phys ed today."

"Oh, you were playing sports." She paused for a moment, set down her knitting and gave him a thumbs-up.

"Make sure to tell your father. He'll be happy to hear it. And you'll be happy to know I'm doing away with the Shame-shelf in that upstairs closet." Then she paused, turning kinda pink and shy. "I apologize. I was wrong. It's not a good thing—Shame. The only *shame* is not being a good person and not respecting yourself and others. That doll. I thought it would discourage you, putting it up there." She laughed.

"I don't know what I was thinking. 'My bad'. Lesson learned. So. Let's just say it's like an action figure. In a dress. Okay? Anything you want to play with is fine with your father and me. Unless you start doing drugs or toting a gun. That's no good. You know we love you, Dan, and want all the best for you and your sister. So go right ahead, play with that doll if it makes you happy. The world is a big place and life is too short… and uh, I spoke with that teacher of yours—the art teacher Mr. Oates."

"Oh."

"Yes. Well, I spoke with him and, uhm—if-"

She abruptly stopped talking.

Danny waited for her to finish but she didn't say anything.

"Mom? 'And if' what?"

"Well… if you're gay. That's okay, too. We love you no matter what."

Danny sat there and wondered what to say.

"I'm a hyphenate, Mom"

Janet seemed confused.

"Who said? Where did you hear that?"

"This girl in my class. Stella. She said I was a hyphenate."

"Well, I agree. You have many talents—but a hyphenate, it's not the same as being gay."

"I don't know what I am, Mom. Do I have to tell you right now? Can I wait awhile?"

Janet picked up her knitting and smiled.

"Sure. We'll be here."

"And the doll—I won't take it anymore. I just liked the story and all. My homeroom teacher said it was artistic. I didn't mean to start a big thing." They sat for a minute then Danny spoke up again.

"So, Mom…what's up with Becky? Why did she shave her eyebrows."

His mother took a breath and set her knitting aside. "Your sister is going through a bad time. This Mark boy has caused all sorts of confusion. She will calm down soon enough. Don't worry about it. She'll come around. I just hope she doesn't show up with a tattoo. That's nothing you're interested in, right Dan?"

Danny couldn't even stand to get a vaccination much less have ink pummeled into his skin by a million tiny needles.

"No, Mom."

He didn't think the *Batman* logo temporary rub-on last year counted since it came off the next day in the tub anyway.

24

When your life's going wrong.
When the fates are unkind.
When you're limping along
and get kicked from behind;
Tell yourself how lucky you are.
Why decry a cloudy sky?
An empty purse,
A crazy universe.
My philosophy is simply:
   things could be worse.
So be happy you're here.
Think of life as a thrill.
And if worse comes to worse
(as we all know it will)
Thank your lucky star you've gotten this far
And tell yourself how lucky you are.

   That's the song from Seussical—no exclamation
point—though I guess you could put one in if you
wanted to.

Danny liked to copy and write out the words to something he was learning in his notebook to help himself remember it better. He didn't think it counted as plagiarism, but would check with Andrea just in case.

Mr. V told him he was now singing his own song and the "Football Hero" song with Mark Going. So that'd be two songs in the show, which was funny because Danny had only ever played a goat in that Christmas pageant and now Andrea was telling him he was going to be a star (exclamation point!).

They were in the lunchroom. It was Vegan Pizza Day again but Andrea had brought a salad from home.

"It's called a Cobb Salad. It's named after some guy named Cobb who invented it. Chicken and veggies and stuff. My mom wants me to eat more greens. It's okay but I wouldn't mind a few bacon bits. You're going to be the star of the Spring Musicale. Nobody else has two songs, right?"

"Well, it's really just one and a half because the other one is with Mark Going. So I share that one."

"Aren't you even a little mad they stole your song? I mean, also it was *my* idea."

Andrea was still upset about that whole turn of events.

"Well, I have the other one and I guess Mark has to do this or they were gonna totally expel him. I think his Dad talked to the school board or something."

Andrea rolled her eyes. "Jocks. Okay, whatever, but you're still onstage a lot. It's practically your own show… So, can Mark Going sing at all? What does he sound like?" She chewed a carrot stick in anticipation.

"Well, it's hard to tell. He's not very loud and stands kinda stiff. Like a giant robot Lego. We're supposed to move around and stuff."

Losing interest in the salad, Andrea plucked out a spinach leaf and tore it into tiny bits as her gaze drifted toward the windows.

"So, you have choreography—that's what they call dancing when you're in a show."

"We just have to run and jump around like we're playing football."

"Well, that's one thing Mark Going can do, at least. Can you? Maybe watch a movie or something."

"I think I can figure it out. We have to rehearse together. Do you believe it?"

"I guess you'll have to call a 'truce' with him. Make peace."

Andrea stared at Danny as he picked the olives off his pizza.

"Olives always look like bugs to me. We have to practice together tomorrow in the music room."

"On Saturday? Maybe you should take a chaperone, you know, for protection."

"Mr. V will be there, so I guess it'll be okay."

Andrea shook her head. "Oooh, listen to you: it's *Mr. V* now!"

"That's what the other kids in the show call him. It's shorter than saying his whole name all the time."

"Well, I like your solo. I listened to it on iTunes. It's cute."

"Yeah, that one from *Seussical*. I think it'll be okay."

"I think it'll be more than okay. I think it'll be great!"

Andrea was a good "pepper-upper," as his grandma liked to say.

25

Becky lay on her bed. Bob had given her a *Fairies & Unicorns* coloring book with strict instructions to de-stress. She had now started calling her parents by their first names of Bob and Janet to intentionally aggravate them, which it did. How dare they treat her like a child?

Bob said he'd read in an article that coloring books were considered good therapy and a calming mindful activity. It came with six color crayon markers and why was she was being treated like this?

It was humiliating. Coloring books?!

Give me a break.

What's next—Mad Libs?

Give me a break.

Pulling the strings of her Hello Kitty knit cap between her teeth, she chewed them while contemplating her eventual escape from the tyranny of family life and the endless boredom that was Milford Haven. Oh, this place! All the houses looked the same and all the streets were named after flowers or trees or presidents. Please! Everything everywhere was so lame. And the drama!

Her little brother was ruining everything with Mark and just being a total pain. She didn't exactly hate him but she couldn't wait until she was in high school next fall with mature kids her own age who didn't have annoying little brothers messing up their social life and ruining their boyfriend's reputation. She rolled over, sat up and turned to the mirror. Omigod is that a pimple? No, it's just a weird reflection. Some kind of shadow. Why can't everything be perfect? She touched her chin, squinting at the newly shaved brows and wondered how it would look if she drew them in. So she picked up the purple crayon marker and carefully lined new eyebrows where the old ones used to be. She stared at herself in the mirror and thought that if she saved her allowance and lunch money she could maybe get contact lenses to match. How mega cool would that be…?

✦　✦　✦　✦　✦

Danny's dad was driving him to rehearsal. It was cold for spring and Danny could see his breath on the window. He drew a smiley face.

"How's the play going?"

"It's not a play really. There's songs. It's a musical. *Musicale*. Mr. V—Mr. Van Horn—says that's the 'old English' spelling. With the 'e' at the end. That's what they used to call them back then. I don't know why."

They sat silent for a moment then his dad flicked the heater on.

"Chilly, huh?"

"Yeah. No more snow at least."

"But it's Ohio, so who knows? I heard you're singing with that boy Mark. I hope he's stopped the bullying. Has he?"

"Yeah, pretty much. The principal made him stop and now he's in the show. They were almost gonna kick him out. That's why he has to sing."

"Well, that's good then. I'm looking forward to your show. Singing is a good thing. I sang karaoke at your Mom's and mine wedding. Uncle Bill was the D.J."

"Do you miss Uncle Bill, Dad?" Danny sure did.

"Yeah, all the time. But you honor someone even when you just even think about them. Their memory. You know, when your Uncle Bill and I were kids, we used to fool around— you know, fight, wrestle, what have you—and one day we were walking home from school and a bird pooped on my head. You know, the white stuff that's all sticky and all. It was summer so my head was bare and the poop just plopped right onto my hair. It was disgusting but your uncle thought it was hilarious. He was my big brother and I always kind of looked up to him and there he was laughing and pointing at me with bird poop on my head. But you know what: there's an ancient belief that when a bird poops on your head, it's good luck. And all I can say is that I've been a lot luckier than most— especially your Uncle Bill, you know? Sometimes what feels like a bad thing turns out to be luckier than you think."

Danny's father pulled up to the curb.

"Well, here we are." There was an awkward pause then his dad continued. "Look, I know you took that doll again, brought it here to school. Your mother told me." He rubbed his hand over his face.

"You have to understand that other kids would give you a hard time. Kids can be mean. Not everybody is your family. I know that even we have trouble sometimes. We try to understand but, well—you have to figure it out for yourself, you know—So... is this a forever deal, this doll business, or what?"

Danny sat for a moment and thought then said "I don't think so, Dad. It was just for that Show-and-Tell day. I told mom I'm not gonna take it anymore. It was just a thing..."

Bob cocked his head to one side quizzically. "A thing, huh?" He smiled a little and laid his hand on Danny's head. "Okay. Whatever you say. What time should I pick you up?"

"I guess about three. It's Saturday so we don't stay too late. Thanks, Dad."

"Sure, Dan-o. Sing good."

Danny grabbed his backpack and got out of the car as his dad honked, waved, and drove away.

26

The hallway was deserted when Danny entered the building. The door made a loud echo as it clicked behind him. The whole place looked like it was waiting for the zombie apocalypse. Empty, quiet, scary.

The building was open so the maintenance guy Ken or somebody had to be here but Danny didn't see anyone. Mr. V had keys and was supposed to be here, too. Danny walked past the showcases near the gym. This was where the school kept all the trophies the sports teams had won. Did they give trophies for musicales? Danny wondered. He'd never seen one. He walked to the end of the hall toward the music room when he heard what sounded like someone singing through the double doors.

Danny crept up and looked inside. He was shorter than the window so had to stand tiptoe. He didn't see Mr. V but Mark Going was there sitting on the piano bench, his ear buds in, singing—or trying to—along with his iPod. Then he got up and started moving around, sort of bouncing and jumping and doing karate kicks to the music. He was singing the football hero song and doing that "choreography" like Andrea called it. It was pretty funny. He really did look like some kind of human Lego. Danny thought that maybe he should just barge in there and call out "Hey Bernadette!" when he heard footsteps behind him coming down the hall.

"Ready for the lion's den, Daniel?"

Danny spun around and nearly fell over. It was Mr. V.

"I think we're safe. He's outnumbered."

Mr. V was carrying a large notebook with a bunch of music sheets shoved inside.

"I know you feel like we cheated with your 'Football Hero' song, giving it to Mark, but desperate times call for desperate measures. He's not exactly playing on home turf. It's all part of the bigger picture. For the good of the show, as they say."

"Okay, yeah. I still get to sing part of it, anyway."

Danny felt flush. He had never spoken to Mr. V or any teacher about much more than a note from the doctor or homework.

Mr. V smiled. "That's the spirit. You're a real trouper."

Danny wondered what that meant. He had never even been a Cub Scout.

Mr. V opened the door and ushered Danny through. "Let's get in there and start to work, shall we? I want you boys to shake hands and come out singing!"

They walked into the room and Mark didn't even see them. Then Mr. V dropped his notebook on purpose, making a loud 'bang'. Mark jumped and jerked around, yanking the ear buds out of his head.

"Oh man, you scared me!"

"Good to see you working, Mark. Now, here's your other half. Let's start at the beginning, shall we?" They all stood there for a minute then Mr. V walked over to the piano, sounded a single note and Danny stepped forward.

"Are you ready boys? Let's see where we're at."

Danny and Mark looked at each other.

"Let's take it from the top. The beginning."

Mr. V began the song. Danny kept time with the music and started to sing. He'd only practiced at home in his room a little but knew the song from the tryouts before. Mark hesitated then hum-mumbled along.

"Louder please, Mark. If you need to hold the music, do that."

Mark clutched the wrinkled sheets from his gym bag and held them tight.

"Now on the chorus, I want you both to meet center stage."

Mark just stood there, his legs shaking.

"The chorus. That's the part you sing together."

Mr. V got up and taking Mark by the shoulders, moved him across the floor.

Mark pulled away and threw the music down.

"I can't do this! I can't do it! This whole thing sucks!"

He stomped to the windows and dropped his head against the glass.

Mr. V stepped over to him and said, "Look Mark, there's a reason you've been given this assignment."

"I know. Punishment." He jammed his head against the window pane, slamming his fist at his side.

"For what?" asked Mr. V.

"I know! For bullying."

"Yes, that's right."

Mr. V and the two boys just stood there then Mark turned to Danny and yelled out "I'm sorry, okay! I'm sorry for getting on your case. I'm sorry for calling you names and pushing you and all that stuff. I wish I'd never heard of Bernadette Peters!"

Mr. V stood behind him. "Well, that's a start anyway. Now what?"

Danny watched as Mark lifted his head, slowly walked over, unclenched his fist and stuck out his hand. Danny waited a moment then took it and shook.

"See. That wasn't so hard, was it?" Mr. V walked back to the piano.

"Now, let's all have a deep breath and take it from the top. Again."

Mark stepped back, gathered up the scattered pages, and took his place next to Danny. Mr. V sounded another chord. Danny stood there for a moment then looked up at Mark and decided to smile.

27

When Danny walked outside to meet his dad, now his mom and Becky were in the car, too. What's going on? They hadn't all been in the car at the same time since like Christmas. Becky didn't even admit to having parents if she could get away with it. Once, when she got grounded, for revenge she told the school clerk she was an "emaciated minor." She was always messing up words like that. Her dad was furious when the principal called last fall after she had appeared in the attendance office with that story.

"You are not an emancipated, emaciated, or any other kind of minor! You are a *major* pain-in-the-butt, is what you are!"

And now she was calling their parents "Bob" and "Janet" and getting on everybody's nerves.

"Hey Dan, how was the singing?" His dad was smiling like The Joker and sounded like a game show host. So what was up?

"We're having a family night at the mall. Hop in."

Becky was slouched in the corner of the back seat, glaring and playing with her hair. Staring at her reflection on the phone and rolling her eyes, she said "Whoopee" then popped her gum.

Danny climbed in next to her, slipped his seat belt on and took a deep breath. "Okay..."

His mom turned around and smiled. "There's a craft fair at the mall this weekend and I thought it'd be nice to have dinner and see what they've got going on there. After all, you did make a basket!"

She winked at Danny, laughed and nodded to Bob.

"Yeah, I heard about that. Good job. Wish I coulda been there for the big moment. Sorry I missed it, Dan-o."

"It just kind of happened but it was pretty cool Dad, yeah."

Becky let out a huge sigh and mumbled "*Cool*. Yeah, right."

Bob whistled and said "But you did it. *You*. I think it's time we shot some hoops together someday soon, whaddaya say, Dan-o?"

Danny hesitated then said "Uhm. Yeah. Okay."

The Mall at Milford was the only hangout for kids anywhere around.

There was Zippo's, which was a new hot dog and burger place that always had bikers on their motorcycles out front and seemed to be attracting what his mom called a "rough crowd." But a lot of the restaurants and storefronts inside the mall were empty or boarded up. Felix's dad owned a really good taco stand in the food court so they went there a lot.

"I think we'll eat at Ale & Olive. How's that, guys?"

Danny's dad loved that place because it had Endless, 'All-You-Can-Eat' Everything. "Your Uncle Bill and I got thrown out of there once for taking too many plates. False advertising! When someplace says 'All-You-Can-Eat,' they better mean it. But there's a new manager now and he's a buddy of mine."

"I'm not crazy about that place, Bob. The food's too rich."

Janet offered an alternative. "I think Salad Sensations is nice and healthy. How about it, guys?"

No one spoke, then Danny said "That sounds good, Mom."

Becky let out another sigh and murmured "No thanks. I'm on a diet."

"You are not on any kind of diet, young lady. You'll eat at the table with the rest of us." Bob pulled the car into a space on the lot and cheerily announced "Here we are."

Salad Sensations was at the north end of the mall and never seemed to have many customers. Danny remembered when they opened. There were carrot-shaped balloons and somebody dressed as a giant celery stalk standing in front handing out coupons for free smoothies.

"This area of the state is a food desert."

Stella always talked about how Ohio lacked ready access to produce. "We're landlocked. Our access to fresh produce is severely limited. That's why places like this are important. What we need is more farmers markets. I'm starting a petition online." But for now Salad Sensations would have to do.

Everything was all-natural. The tables were wood and the chairs were 100% recycled plastic. The walls were green and yellow and so was the food. They did have gluten free Jell-O which was good. Danny had a veggie burger. Becky had tofurkey soup and some pita chips with spinach dip. Danny's dad had a soy (fakin') bacon, lettuce and tomato sandwich and his mom had a kale and quinoa salad.

"Sensational", she said. Then there were some yogurt cookies. When they were done his dad said "Next time: ribs."

The mall was bustling with activity so the family headed over toward the south end where the Craft Fair was in full swing. Danny's parents were chatty and attentive at the booths while Becky slumped behind, checking her cellphone by the second for some hoped-for text or super-important call. There were all kinds of what his dad said were "ethnocentric" artists displaying their wares. There were Native American artifacts collected at the booths as well as local Midwestern landscape paintings and some Amish and Southern handicrafts. A cluster of Hindu textiles hung outside a tent. There were mini-Eskimo mudhut doorstops and lots of blankets and jewelry, furnishings and housewares.

"How many potholders does one person need?" Danny's dad winced a little when his mom picked up a bundle of a half-dozen potholders woven from flax seeds and hemp.

"Look at the beading. All those tiny stitches. I won't use them, they're too fine. It's up on the wall with these."

Bob pointed out an American Girl kiosk that Becky showed an almost violent disinterest in. ("What am I—Five?!")

Danny wandered over to the end of a row of booths where a sign was posted for "The Pious Artisan." He saw dozens of carved wooden and marble boxes of various sizes laid out with price tags and note cards that read "Certificate of Authenticity." Lingering at the booth, Danny asked the man behind the table what that meant.

"That means they are what they say they are. Authentic, true, made-by-hand from rare wood and stone by me. Guaranteed."

The man was older, like maybe in college or something, and was wearing a poncho with a long braid of hair down his back. He wore some silver rings and a few bracelets on his arms which were (uh-oh!) tattooed.

"What's a Pious Artisan?" Danny asked.

"That's me. I'm the Pious Artisan. Do you know what those words mean? I'm pious because I'm devoted to God and I make art so I am an artisan. Get it?"

Danny stared at the boxes on the table.

He picked one up and held it to the light. "What would I put in this?"

The smooth marble surface shone. "Anything you want," the man said.

"Everyone is an artisan in their own way. Life is art. I just happen to believe in God's way. All my pieces honor him."

Danny had seen people on TV saying "God's word," preaching and stuff, and they always seemed loud or angry, phony. His family didn't go to church or anything, but his grandparents did. He wondered if he was missing something.

"Well, I guess that means that you're authentic, right?"

Danny set the box down and wondered if he was authentic, too.

I'm only almost eleven, he thought, maybe I have time. Just then he heard his mom calling from across the mall to come see the dolls constructed out of locally farmed corn husks and strawflowers.

◆ ◆ ◆ ◆ ◆

Later that night, Danny's mom asked how the rehearsal with Mark had gone. "How did it go today, Dan, with that boy Mark?"

"Okay. Mr. V was there so we just sang the song and danced a little."

"I hope you are being conciliatory."

"Uhm, I think so. What's that?"

"That means you are being a good person, an adult."

"But I'm not an adult."

His mom stopped for a moment, then smiled at him and winked.

"I know, but you can practice by overlooking that boy's past bad behavior and try making a new start."

A "truce," like Andrea said.

"He apologized and said he was sorry."

"Well, that's good to hear."

"But he's still pretty lame—his singing at least."

"All the more reason for you to be your best self. Not everyone is good at everything. You have talents that he doesn't and he's a good—what, athlete and such, right? I'm sure if you asked he could help you with that basketball playing just like you can help him with this show."

Wow.

His mom was talking really hardcore.

She sounded like what Tommy Kessler called a "shrink." When Tommy's parents got divorced they started sending him to this doctor to help him adjust to the "structural changes in his family of origin."

Or something like that.

"My Mom calls him a 'talking doctor' but he's really a shrink. He's called a 'talking doctor' 'cause he helps you feel better by talking. He says I have to be patient and loving and that my parents are people too, and that it's all right to cry. I'm supposed to be the one talking but he talks way more than me. I guess it's a good thing but I hate it when grown-ups fight. And now my Dad has a new wife and I have a new baby brother—I just wish I was old then I wouldn't have to go back and forth between my parents. But I have a ton of air miles and they got me a new puppy last Christmas. I named him Delta. It's all good."

28

"So, there's a benefit car wash this weekend to raise money for the future-student-something-or others to go to Washington DC this summer and I'll be there with Mark."

Becky was talking to Misty in New Mexico.

"They're letting him do it 'cause it's for a good cause. It's gonna be our first real date in like *forever*. Well, two weeks. I have to sneak out like a criminal because my parents don't want me to see him 'cause my little brother squealed on him for some ridiculous—that I can't even—don't—I can't even…"

The benefit car wash was an annual event held for a different student group every spring. Last year, the band went to music camp for a week in the Catskills. The Catskills had nothing to do with cats or killing, which was a relief to Danny. They are a mountain range in upstate New York.

"New York—that's where Broadway is."

Andrea was giving a short lecture on U.S. geography.

"In Manhattan, where my cousin moved. It's also called The Big Apple."

Danny waited to make sure she was finished then asked if she was going to the car wash.

"I don't want to get my hair wet. It'll frizz out. I'll go with you and watch, though."

Danny wasn't sure if he was going. "I don't know. Maybe I'll go if you will."

So they went. The sun was out and it was as warm as summer.

Andrea wore a big hat that looked like a flying saucer.

"I know you don't like hats, but not me. I love them. The bigger, the better. You should see my aunts. We're the Von *Hat* Family!"

The maintenance guy Ken was there and a couple of firemen who were supervising with some of the teachers. Matt Ross got sent home for turning a hose on two girls and trying to start a wet t-shirt contest.

("Hey dudes, chill—it's only water.")

Andrea pulled Danny aside when they saw Becky and Mark across the parking lot wiping down the windshield of an SUV.

"Look who's here. I thought they were grounded." So did Danny.

He wondered if Becky would get in his face or just ignore him.

Then he saw her walking towards them. Andrea stood by watching and biting a hangnail. Becky stopped right in front of Danny, staring him down. Then she sort of smiled.

"Mark—my boyfriend—is really sorry for bullying you and calling you names. He told me to tell you that he's super excited about the show and that he hopes that you can both get along now, okay? They said we could be here 'cause it's for a good cause." She paused and pulled her hair into a knot. "So how's that?"

Danny half-smiled and didn't know what to say.

"Well? Are you gonna tell on me now?"

He stared back at her. "No, I guess."

"Okay, then." Becky turned, said "Thanks" over her shoulder and walked back to where Mark was vacuuming out a town car.

Andrea mouthed a silent "Wow" and stared at Danny. "So?"

"So—what?"

"Well, that doesn't really count, you know. *He's* the one that's supposed to apologize."

"He already did. At rehearsal. Mr. V made him. He said he was sorry. So I don't want to think about it anymore."

"Why not?" Andrea shook her head and her hat flopped around. "I wouldn't trust him. I mean he might not be done. He could start cyber-bullying and stalk-texting you next."

"No, he won't. He's afraid of cellphones. He thinks they give you cancer."

Andrea burst out laughing.

"OMG, you're kidding. How do you know that? Who said?"

"My mom told me."

"What a laugh! Mr. Big Deal Jock is afraid of cellphones. Some bully."

"And besides, I don't even have a phone."

"Well, you should get one. I mean, they're good for emergencies."

"My parents said I could on my next birthday."

"And then make fun of Mark Going like he does you."

"No. My mom says I have to be an adult."

"But you're not an adult. You're ten and a half!"

"Almost eleven."

"Still. He's more of an adult than you are."

"I know, that's what I said."

"Well, I guess that's one way to do it, but it sure would be karma."

Karma?

Andrea explained. "Karma is invisible energy you put out that comes back to you—good or bad. It's Buddhist. My cousin does yoga and stuff."

"Well, I just want to do this show and then forget all about Mark Going, okay?"

29

The Spring Musicale was three days away and everybody was excited and kinda scared.

"I'm kinda scared." Amber Tucker was especially nervous. "Well, excited *and* scared. I brought my Pillow Pet." She had recovered from her upper-respiratory ailment and "I couldn't sing or talk or anything for like two weeks. They weren't sure what I had. It was a mystery. They almost didn't think I'd make it. I'm not supposed to have too much stress, though. My immune system is depressed."

She was singing a song called 'Hey, Look Me Over (exclamation point!)' and drinking green tea with honey and lemon all the time. "I'm now totally addicted. I have to have it or I can't even exist. I just hope I can hold up 'til the show. It's on my Bucket List."

Danny stared at her.

"You know—things to do before I die."

"Are you really bad sick?"

"You're so cute, you looked all like—oooh! just now. No. *Bucket List*—it's just a saying. You know, a thing people say... I also want to become a YouTube sensation."

Danny didn't have a Bucket List but was only thinking about summer vacation and getting a fish. His parents said he could get a fish since his mom was allergic to animal fur. He would finally have a pet again.

Danny had a turtle in third grade but he fed it oatmeal once by mistake and it died. His name was Teddy. Danny used to think about Teddy and how turtles are

soooooooooo slow

and stuff

and how he

felt like

a turtle

sometimes.

It seemed like everything took so long to happen and when it did he wondered if it was worth waiting for.

And now Mr. V told him that he had to wear a helmet for his duet with Mark because it was the football song.

Having anything on his head made him itchy and nervous. He felt trapped and hated it and "the helmet will cover my ears. I won't be able to hear."

Mr. V dismissed his fears. "We'll just have to find something that fits. I'll check with the coach."

His dad said they could buy one and he could use it for the song then save it for later if Danny decided he wanted to play football in high school.

"Dream on, Bob. Our son is not playing football anytime, anywhere."

Danny's mom was firm.

"He's not interested in sports and I'm not letting him get his brains bashed in. No way. Forget it."

Then the day before the show, Felix came up to Danny at his locker and made him an offer. "You can use one of mine. I have like twelve helmets. And we've pretty much got the same size head." Felix took a ruler out of his backpack and measured Danny's head from his hair to his chin. Then he made a circle with his hands and put them around the top, what Felix called the "crown."

"Almost exactly perfect."

So the next day Felix brought Danny a Miami Dolphins helmet.

Danny liked that it was a fish. Andrea corrected him. "Dolphins are mammals—but they look and swim like fish, so whatever."

Felix held the helmet up to the light. "I brought you a newer one that's not so smelly. I put animal team logo stickers on all my helmets. I want to be a zoologist when I grow up." Felix showed Danny how to put the helmet on without crushing his head and helped him adjust the chin strap so it wasn't too tight.

"It's just for make believe, right?" Felix laughed. "You're not gonna get tackled or anything, unless that Mark guy goes nuts."

Danny didn't feel as itchy and trapped by the helmet as he thought he would. There was rubber padding on the inside and it wasn't so bad.

Later that day he modeled it for Andrea.

"Wow. You look good. I like the colors. Welcome to the wonderful world of headgear. Now you should get a beret. That's what artists wear. It's French."

30

"Rise and shine." Danny felt a tugging on his toes.

"Time to wake up."

Danny didn't want to.

"It's the Big Day!"

Oh, yeah, Danny thought. The *show*.

He opened one eye. His mom stood at the foot of the bed.

"I made your favorite for breakfast—blueberry pancakes!"

Danny could smell them but didn't want pancakes or anything else. He just wanted to stay in bed under the covers but his mom was standing over him looking all gigantic and smiling so he decided to get up and go.

◆　◆　◆　◆

That night at the show all the families and friends were there.

Andrea sat in the front row with her mom. She clapped the whole time but you couldn't really hear it because she was wearing gloves a lot now to keep her from biting her nails so much. She brought Danny a big silver balloon shaped like a star that said "Congrats! You're a Star!"

Earlier that day Andrea had shown Danny a Skype message to him from the real, actual Bernadette Peters. "I wrote her a secret note and sent it to the theatre in New York and she got it. I told her about the show and that you were her biggest fan and invited her to come see it. I didn't tell you 'cause I wanted it to be a surprise. She couldn't be here but she sent this to you personally, she says your name and everything. She looks even better than her picture."

Danny watched it and said it was a nice thing to do. It made him happy to know that a big Broadway star knew his name. And she was pretty, too.

Andrea was gloating. "Maybe we should show it to Jock-o just to make him jealous."

Like Mark Going would've even cared. Not.

"Remember to check the running order of the songs and keep track of your place. Older kids help the little ones."

Some of the younger kids in the show were from the elementary school so Mr. V had assigned Miss Mathers to be backstage and tell everybody what to do. There was a sheet posted on the wall with all the songs listed of who sang what and when.

Danny and Mark's song was second to last following Mindy and Mandy Mills. They were identical twins, always wore matching everything and liked to trick people 'cause they looked alike.

"We were born a minute apart. I'm older." Mindy's favorite color was purple and Mandy liked pink. They were singing a song called "Together Wherever We Go."

"That's our motto."

The day before, Danny's solo song 'How Lucky You Are' had gotten canceled because the show was running too long and everybody had to have at least one chance to sing.

His dad said sometimes things don't go the way you planned.

Mr. V said "That's show-biz, kid!"

Miss Mathers lined Danny up behind the curtain.

"You boys are next."

Mark was supposed to come on from the other side and meet in the middle but Danny didn't see him.

"Where's Mark?"

Miss Mathers looked over but didn't see him either.

"Oh my, let me check."

Danny was nervous and biting his lip. He was so nervous he almost started laughing. Maybe Mark had chickened out at the last minute. It was dark backstage and hard to see. Oh no, he thought, this is just like my dream... Now what?

Then he heard Mrs. Cooney play the beginning of the 'Football Hero' song. He had his helmet on and decided to go out anyway. He was ready even if Mark wasn't.

'Fortune favors the bold.' That's what Mr. Oates said. Okay...

He took a deep breath. Mrs. Cooney played the beginning music again and Danny trotted onstage and started singing.

The lights were bright and in his eyes. Everything else was dark. He could hear the music but it sounded far away. He couldn't see the people but felt them sitting and breathing.

Some of them coughed. He looked offstage. Danny sang his part louder so they maybe wouldn't notice that Mark was missing. Then all of a sudden there were frantic punches from behind the backstage curtain. First an arm then a knee then all of Mark Going ran out pulling on his helmet. He tripped on a shoelace, looked terrified and like a total goon but Danny kept singing. Mark was standing with his back to the audience and flubbed some lines then hummed that part and Danny had to fill in the words. A few of the people laughed so Danny started doing football moves and pushing Mark the right way around. Everything seemed to be happening in slow-motion. It was like a really weird alien universe gym class.

Then it was all over. The song ended, the people clapped, Danny bowed and Mark ran offstage.

Cameron Briggs was last. He was the youngest kid and pretty small for his age anyway. Cameron was singing "Getting Tall" from Nine but "I'm only seven and short. My mom says that's irony."

The ending finale song was everybody coming onstage to sing "Always Look on the Bright Side of Life" from Spamalot.

After the show, Mark gave Danny a high-five, said "Legendary, bro" then got sprayed by his buddies with Gatorade in the parking lot. But he still looked like a Lego.

Danny was shaking but it was the good, happy kind. Like at Christmas or when he got a great surprise birthday present or that basket in phys ed. He looked around, at all the people and everything seemed the same, just like it was before.

Stella was there and gave him a rose.

Andrea glitter-bombed him then they posed for a selfie.

And Felix let him keep the helmet so he could practice wearing it at home.

He saw his parents waving thumbs-up above the crowd. His dad said, "Great job, Dan-o."

His mom said, "We're so proud."

But Danny felt different. It was like he was up in a plane. He'd only been in a plane twice and both times he never looked out the window during the flight. But now he felt like he was looking down on the world, seeing the whole thing from a higher place. He'd been on the ferris wheel at carnivals, too. Sometimes the ride stopped at the top to let the people at the bottom get off. His Uncle Bill would rock the seat and Danny would be frightened that they'd fall but they never did. "Don't worry, Dragonfruit. Never fear. I got you. I'll always have you, buddy."

Things happen or they don't. People you cared about could go away and you had to keep on doing what you did the day before like going to school and brushing your teeth. He didn't know if he liked it yet but now Danny felt a little better, braver and surer, too. I guess growing up is something everybody has to do.

◆　◆　◆　◆　◆

Mark Going never apologized publicly like he was supposed to because the assembly got canceled at the last minute due to a suspicious unclaimed brown paper package. The whole building had to be evacuated then everybody got to go home for the day. Like a lot of stuff, it was scary at first but then okay.

The suspicious package turned out to be a box of two hundred cloth baby diapers that one of the lunch ladies had left in the kitchen.

In June, right after graduation, Mark and his family moved away from Milford Haven when his dad got a job transfer to Texas.

Becky told everybody they were still going together and that lots of people have long-distance relationships but then met Matt Ross's older brother who was almost sixteen and decided she liked him better.

"He's really fun at parties and is doing Outward Bound in Wyoming this summer when he graduates. Then we're going to Mardi Gras!"

He didn't and they didn't.

Her parents got her a tutor to help with her classes and an iPad. Danny got one too and he and Andrea started talking online even though they saw each other practically every day. When Danny got his new pet fish, they brainstormed for a name.

"A fish can be a spirit animal, right?"

Danny thought that since he had the fish he might as well give it something to do. A purpose in life.

Andrea thought for a minute. "Sure. I guess. It's better than a rat or a snake—yuck! But I thought you wanted a dragon."

"I'm kinda over dragons so-"

"So, what're you gonna call him? He has to have a name."

"But not a nickname!" Danny had decided—no more nicknames.

Andrea peered through the glass. "Do we know for sure if it's a boy or what?"

Danny hadn't thought of that. "How do you tell?"

"Does it matter with a fish? I mean, what can he do, he's in there alone."

They stared at the fish in the bowl swimming around the plastic coral and fake seaweed, resting on pebbles and catching food flakes in its mouth.

"He looks happy. I guess it can be whatever you want it to be."

Danny thought for a minute.

"A boy or a girl?"

Andrea nodded her approval. "Or just a fish. Anything you want. I mean, it's yours."

STEVEN KEYES is a native of Chicago by way of Texas and New York. An actor as well as writer, his play *Moonlight Cocktail* was produced in Los Angeles and his solo show *West of Eden* in New York. He has appeared off-Broadway, in regional theatre, national tours, TV and film. For five years he mentored at the Virginia Avenue Project and his writing has been published by Samuel French, Smith & Kraus, and Applause Books. He studied with Wynn Handman at the American Place Theatre and Columbia University.

Made in the USA
Las Vegas, NV
23 May 2021